The Consumption Function in Economics

Stavros A. Drakopoulos

The Consumption Function in Economics

History, Method and Policy Implications

palgrave
macmillan

Stavros A. Drakopoulos
Department of History and Philosophy of Science
National and Kapodistrian University
Athens, Greece

ISBN 978-3-032-15957-1 ISBN 978-3-032-15958-8 (eBook)
https://doi.org/10.1007/978-3-032-15958-8

This Palgrave Macmillan imprint is published by the registered company Springer Nature Switzerland AG.
The registered company address is: Gewerbestrasse 11, 6330 Cham, Switzerland

To my students

Acknowledgements

Several colleagues have helped me directly and indirectly in writing this short monograph, but special thanks are due to Peter Earl who read the whole manuscript at the final pre-publication stage. I gratefully acknowledge his extremely helpful and thoughtful insights and suggestions regarding many sections of the work. I also wish to express my sincere thanks to Ioannis Katselidis who read the whole manuscript and provided a number of useful comments and identified some important omissions. I am grateful to George Gotsis who suggested suitable references regarding the historical part of the work. I have benefited from discussions with Thomas Moutos who pointed to some key works that helped me clarify many points, especially with respect to modern developments in macroeconomics.

Many other colleagues have also contributed indirectly through conferences, seminars, personal discussions, and comments to my works. Acknowledgements are due to Lawrence Boland, Roger Backhouse, José Luís Cardoso, Till Dupe, Sheila Dow, Arne Heise, Maurice Lagueux, Marc Lavoie, Robert McMaster, George Panos, Daria Pignalosa, Louis-Philippe Rochon, Sergio Rosi, Ioannis Theodossiou, Alex Thomas, Attilio Trezzini, and Yannis Venieris.

I would also like to thank the following colleagues working in Universities in Greece who have helped me through discussions in conferences, meetings, and personal communications: Chrys Mantzavinos, Theodor Mariolis, Michael Psalidopoulos, Stathis Psillos, Kostis Reppapis, Nicholas Theocarakis, Lefteris Tsoulfidis, Aristotle Tympas, and Michel Zouboulakis. Many thanks are also due to Wyndham Hacket Pain, Senior

Editor, Economics for Palgrave Macmillan for encouraging me to write this book and for his support through the period of writing. Finally, thanks are due to the anonymous referees who made extremely useful comments and suggestions regarding the initial book proposal. All mistakes, misrepresentations, and deficiencies remain the sole responsibility of the author.

Parts of some sections of this book draw from material that has appeared in the form of a Journal paper published in 2021 in the *European Journal of the History of Economic Thought*, vol. 28, No. 6, pp. 965–984; and from a book chapter titled Theories of Consumption as part of a 2021 volume *An introduction to Macroeconomics*, edited by Louis-Philippe Rochon and Sergio Rosi, Edward Elgar, Chentelham, UK, pp. 233–267. Some material of chapter 9 draws from my 2016 article in the *Journal of Philosophical Economics*, vol. 10, No. 1, pp. 28–57.

Competing Interests The author has no competing interests to declare that are relevant to the content of this manuscript.

Summary

Given that consumption expenditures as a share of GDP are around 70 per cent in most advanced economies and even more in less advanced ones, consumption is important for aggregate demand, and the level of output and employment. It is also crucial for aggregate savings, investment, capital stock, and income growth. The history of aggregate consumption studies reveals key theoretical and methodological issues which still reverberate to contemporary consumption theories. The introductory chapter provides the main motivation regarding the central theme of this work which is the history of consumption function and its methodological and economic policy dimensions. The book begins with the origins and the main ideas regarding aggregate consumption before the seminal contribution of John Maynard Keynes and finishes with the latest theoretical and methodological developments on the issue. It places more attention to their conceptual development, attempting to examine also the methodological framework in which consumption theories were devised. Further, the work brings into the fore the important economic policy implications associated to various consumption formulations. In general, the interpretation that is offered here connects the history of consumption function to important methodological developments and to the ensuing shifts in economic policy recommendations.

Contents

1	**General Introduction**	1
	Introduction	1
	Chapter Outlines	5
	References	8
2	**Approaches to Consumption Before Keynes**	11
	Introduction	11
	Veblen: Critique of Marginalism and of Neoclassical Economics	12
	Veblen: Conspicuous Consumption	14
	Hazel Kyrk's Theory of Consumption and Savings	17
	Concluding Comments	19
	References	20
3	**Aggregate Consumption in the Economics of John Maynard Keynes**	25
	Introduction	25
	Keynes' Criticism of Utility Theory	26
	Consumption in Keynes' Economic Thought	28
	The Standard Keynesian Consumption Function Analysis	30
	Concluding Comments	35
	References	35

4 Early Empirical Testing of Consumption Function and the Kuznets' Paradox 39
Introduction 39
Empirical Testing of Keynesian Consumption Function 40
Simon Kuznets and the Consumption Paradox 42
The Early Empirical Dimensions of the Kuznets' Paradox 45
Concluding Comments 47
References 48

5 The Social Significance of Consumption: James Duesenberry and Harvey Leibenstein 51
Introduction 51
James Duesenberry: The Social Significance of Consumption 52
Critique of Fundamental Assumptions of Demand Theory 53
The Relative Income Hypothesis 55
Harvey Leibenstein: Social Status and Consumption 60
Concluding Comments 64
References 65

6 The Emergence of the Neoclassical Consumption Function 69
Introduction 69
Orthodox Reactions to Keynes' and Duesenberry's Consumption Theories 70
Irving Fisher's Theory of Intertemporal Choice 73
The Life-Cycle Hypothesis 76
The Permanent-Income Hypothesis 80
Concluding Comments 83
References 84

7 Current Status of the Mainstream Consumption Functions 89
Introduction 89
Rational Expectations and Random Walk Theory of Consumption 90
Empirical Testing and Modifications of the Euler Equation 92
Consumption and DSGE Models 95
Alternatives to the Representative Agent Model 96
Habit Formation, Catching Up, and Keeping Up with the Joneses 98

Concluding Comments 100
References 101

8 Non-mainstream Approaches to Consumption 105
Introduction 105
Keynesian Approaches to Consumption: James Tobin 106
Michal Kalecki and Kaleckian-Based Approaches to Consumption 108
Consumption in the Works of Nicholas Kaldor and Luigi Pasinetti 112
Post Keynesian Approaches to Consumption 114
Concluding Comments 116
References 117

9 The Methodological Framework of Aggregate Consumption Analysis 121
Introduction 121
Contemporary Strands of Mainstream Macroeconomics 122
Microfoundations 123
The Notion of Representative Agent 126
Methodological Individualism 128
Heterodox Macroeconomic Approaches 130
Concluding Comments 133
References 133

10 Policy Implications and Conclusions 139
Introduction 139
Keynes, Duesenberry, and Keynesianism 140
Mainstream Theories Based on Rational Optimising Agents 141
Old Keynesianism, Post Keynesians, and Other Heterodox Schools 144
New Behavioural Economics 145
The Presence of Ideology 147
General Conclusions 148
References 150

Index 155

Abbreviations

ABM:	Agent-Based Models
AIH:	Absolute Income Hypothesis
APC:	Average Propensity to Consume
APS:	Average Propensity to Save
DSGE:	Dynamic Stochastic General Equilibrium
GDP:	Gross Domestic Product
HANK:	Heterogeneous Agent New Keynesian
LCH:	Life-cycle Hypothesis of consumption
MPC:	Marginal Propensity to Consume
MPS:	Marginal Propensity to Save
MRS:	Marginal Rate of Substitution
PIH:	Permanent-Income hypothesis of consumption
RANK:	Representative Agent New Keynesian
RBC:	Real Business Cycle Models
REPIH:	Rational Expectations Permanent Income
RIH:	Relative Income Hypothesis
SIG:	Social Influence Group
TANK:	Two-Agents New Keynesian

List of Figures

Fig. 3.1	The Keynesian consumption function	31
Fig. 3.2	The multiplier effect of a change in autonomous consumption	33
Fig. 4.1	Short-run and long-run consumption functions	44
Fig. 5.1	Duesenberry's long-run and short-run consumption functions	56
Fig. 6.1	Fisher's theory of intertemporal choice	75
Fig. 6.2	The life-cycle hypothesis of consumption	77
Fig. 6.3	Permanent-income hypothesis	82
Fig. 7.1	Consumer optimisation when the borrowing constraint is binding	94

CHAPTER 1

General Introduction

Introduction

Consumption expenditures as a share of GDP are around 70 per cent in most advanced economies and even more in less advanced ones. On the theoretical level, consumption is important for aggregate demand, and the level of output and employment in an economy. Given that income not consumed is saved, the level of savings has a large impact on capital stock, investment, and income growth. Further, the marginal propensity to consume determines the magnitudes of government expenditure and tax multipliers. Thus consumption expenditures are also closely related to the effectiveness of economic policies, and especially of fiscal policy. As John Maynard Keynes declared: “Consumption – to repeat the obvious – is the sole end and object of all economic activity” (Keynes, 1936, p. 104). The systematic analysis of consumption expenditures is therefore a central subject of study in economics discourse with a long presence in the history of economic thought.

The history of aggregate consumption studies reveals key theoretical and methodological issues which still reverberate to contemporary consumption theories. Early ideas regarding the role of aggregate consumption can be found in classical political economy (see, for instance, Fiaschi & Signorino, 2003; Thomas, 2024). The prime example is Thomas Malthus’ notion of underconsumption. According to Malthus, the fundamental obstacle which may hamper economic growth in an industrialised

S. A. Drakopoulos, *The Consumption Function in Economics*,
https://doi.org/10.1007/978-3-032-15958-8_1

economy is the lack of "an adequate stimulus to the continued increase of wealth" (Malthus, 1986 vol. VI, p. 288; Fiaschi & Signorino, 2003). Malthus' underconsumption thesis has had a discernible impact on Keynes' thinking and has been linked to Keynesian theory (e.g. Eltis, 1980; Rutherford, 1987).[1] John Hobson, a self-styled economic heretic, also conceived a theory of underconsumption which was used to explain and analyse economic and social issues such as unemployment (Richmond, 1978). However in most of the early works, aggregate consumption was not the main focus of investigation, but part of a wider framework of economic discourse.

The first systematic studies of aggregate consumption originate in the late nineteenth and early twentieth centuries in the works of Thorstein Veblen (1899a, 1899b) and American Institutional economics (e.g. Kyrk, 1923). One basic feature of these studies was the emphasis on the social dimension of consumption patterns. The next major contribution appeared in the seminal work of Keynes (1936), who integrated an aggregate consumption function to his macroeconomic analysis. In the same manner as the Institutionalists and in accordance to his rejection of the standard utility maximising model of consumers, Keynes stressed the psychological and sociological aspects of consumption decisions. Almost a decade after Keynes, James Duesenberry's (1949) work on consumption was in the same conceptual framework, incorporating the role of sociological and psychological determinants of consumption. Their policy implications were also similar, supporting a strong role of activist economic policy.

In the first decades after WWII and in the context of testing and interpreting empirical findings of US consumption data, the first alternatives to Keynes' consumption function appeared. One major finding was the difference between the long-run and the short-run behaviour of the consumers' consumption patterns, known as the 'Kuznets' Paradox' (Kuznets, 1942). Kuznets' empirical work set the basis for the emergence of alternative consumption functions to the Keynesian formulation. The emerging methodological trend was to ground the consumption function on mainstream microeconomic principles, and especially on the theory of rational consumer. The theory basically involves a particular model of human behaviour that entails forward-looking and utility optimising agents. Irving Fisher's (1930) book on intertemporal choice between present and

[1] For an interesting discussion of the views on consumption found in Keynes and Ricardo, see Thomas, 2025.

future consumption provided the necessary theoretical background. The life-cycle hypothesis of consumption function developed by Franco Modigliani and Richard Brumberg (1954), and the permanent-income hypothesis developed by Milton Friedman (1957), emerged as the two main alternatives to Keynes' and Duesenberry's approaches. The gradual displacement of Keynes' absolute income hypothesis and of the limited appeal of Duesenberry's relative income hypothesis was not based on their theoretical or empirical failure. Their lack of microeconomic foundations and their allegedly psychological and sociological characteristics were deemed to be unacceptable on methodological grounds.

One important feature of the life-cycle and of permanent-income hypotheses was the diminished role of current income in consumption decisions. The role of income was even further diminished with the appearance of 'random walk' consumption theories characterised by rational expectations (Hall, 1978; but also Lucas, 1972; Barro, 1979). As a result and contrary to Keynes and Duesenberry, subsequent consumption theories, which formed the core of New Classical macroeconomics, provided theoretical justification for the very limited role of fiscal policy to smooth out large fluctuations of produced output and employment (see also Bunting, 1989; Palley, 2010).

Most contemporary mainstream consumption formulations are based on the notion of the representative agent or household (RANK models). Agents are assumed to be forward-looking and fully informed utility maximisers and to operate in an environment characterised by calculable uncertainty (Stiglitz, 2018). In those theories, current income plays a minimal role on the level of consumption, mainly because agents engage in consumption smoothing over their expected lifetime (Woodford, 2009; Muellbauer, 2016). The rise of RANK formulations was almost parallel to the gradual emergence of the new neoclassical synthesis, also known as Dynamic Stochastic General Equilibrium (DSGE) theory. In recent years and due to the empirical shortcomings of RANK models, modified versions such as the Heterogeneous Agent New Keynesian (HANK) and the Two-Agents New Keynesian (TANK) emerged.

During the period of the formation of orthodox consumption functions, there were also alternative approaches to aggregate consumption originating from non-mainstream authors and schools of thought. These approaches criticised the basic assumptions and the underlying methodological framework of mainstream consumption functions. The standard or 'Old' Keynesianism (e.g. James Tobin, 1951) was one of those approaches. Another stream of thought was associated with the work of Michael Kalecki (1971) and Kaleckian-based formulations, and with the theoretical views on consumption developed by Nicholas Kaldor (1955–1956) and by Luigi Pasinetti (1962). Furthermore, broad common theoretical and methodological characteristics concerning aggregate consumption can be observed in the contemporary Post Keynesian school of economic thought. The rejection of the concept of representative agent and of the central assumption of optimising behaviour of agents are two prime examples. The role of economic policy for the stabilisation of capitalism was, and still is, another important common feature of the non-mainstream analyses of consumption.

The methodological setting has played a pivotal role in the formation of orthodox approaches to aggregate consumption. This becomes clearer after an examination of the three fundamental components of contemporary mainstream formulations: the notion of microfoundations, the role of the representative agent, and the framework of methodological individualism. Further, the criticisms that have been applied to the above key components by various economists belonging to different intellectual traditions including heterodox macroeconomists also assist in the overall comprehension of the underlying issues pertaining to consumption functions.

There have been a number of journal papers focusing on various aspects of the history of consumption function (e.g. Hynes, 1998; Mason, 2000; Chao, 2003; Deaton, 2005; Edwards, 2014; Todorova, 2014; Trezzini, 2012, 2016; Pignalosa, 2025). There are fewer monographs, with Deaton (1992), and Jappelli and Pistaferri (2017) being the prime examples. The present short monograph follows a largely historical approach to the theoretical development of consumption function, but it does not aim to be a comprehensive historical account of consumption theories. It places more attention to their conceptual development, attempting to examine also the methodological framework in which consumption theories were devised. The work also brings into the fore the important economic policy implications associated to various consumption formulations. Inevitably, the perspective of this book involves some discussion of the history of macroeconomics, especially since Keynes' major work, but it does not focus on such a history. In general, the interpretation that is offered here connects the history of consumption function to important methodological developments and to the ensuing shifts in economic policy recommendations.

Chapter Outlines

After the introduction, Chap. 2 discusses the origins and the main ideas regarding aggregate consumption before the seminal contribution of John Maynard Keynes. It starts with Thorstein Veblen's critique of Marginalism and of early Neoclassical economics and proceeds to his analysis of the notion of conspicuous consumption. Veblen's ideas on consumption were further developed by economists operating in the American institutionalist tradition, and especially by Hazel Kyrk who was a key figure of this tradition regarding the study of consumption. It also briefly presents the views on consumption of women economists in the US, also belonging to the institutionalist school of economic thought. The chapter argues that the fundamental characteristic of all these pre-Keynesian approaches was the emphasis on the social dimension of consumption and the analysis of consumption patterns as a social phenomenon.

Chapter 3 starts with Keynes' criticism of utility theory which was the standard model of decision making of his contemporary orthodoxy. It proceeds with a presentation of the key components of Keynes' approach to aggregate consumption, including his recognition of the psychological and sociological aspects of consumption decisions. The chapter focuses on the notions of the dependence of consumption expenditure on the level of income, and on the absolute income hypothesis. It also elaborates on the notion of the multiplier which is fundamental for the role of fiscal policy in economic stabilisation, especially during recessions. Contrary to subsequent neoclassical consumption theories, Keynes' theory was not based on the standard model of individual rational behaviour. It also discusses the standard Keynesian analysis of aggregate consumption and its significance for the level of output and employment. Finally, the economic policy implications of the Keynesian consumption function will also be briefly presented.

Almost immediately after the publication of Keynes' major work, there were the first attempts to test the Keynesian consumption function and its implications. Chapter 4 starts with an examination of the background of the empirical work relating to the Keynesian consumption function. One major finding was the difference between the long-run and the short-run behaviour of the consumers' consumption patterns, known as the 'Kuznets' Paradox'. It thus proceeds with Simon Kuznets' empirical work on consumption, which set the basis for the emergence of alternative consumption functions to the Keynesian formulation. The chapter finishes with a critical discussion of the early empirical dimensions of the paradox, also focusing on subsequent interpretations of its econometric methodology.

Among the many attempts to explain Kuznets' findings was James Duesenberry's work with the introduction of his *Relative Income Hypothesis* (RIH), a theoretical construction which similar to Veblen and Keynes exhibits a strong psychological and sociological dimension. Chapter 5 commences with a discussion of Duesenberry's hypothesis and proceeds to his critique of the fundamental assumptions of mainstream demand theory. After discussing the main components of his theory including the role of the demonstration and ratchet effects, the key implications of Duesenberry's hypothesis are also considered. The chapter proceeds with a presentation of Harvey Leibenstein's ideas on social status and consumption, who was also working in a similar conceptual framework as Duesenberry. There will also be a brief discussion of George Katona's views who was placing emphasis on the psychological aspects of consumption decisions.

In the early 1950s, the emergence of life-cycle and the permanent-income hypotheses of consumption were the 'mainstream responses' to Keynes' and Duesenberry's consumption theories. Chapter 6 begins with the mainstream attitudes towards the absolute income hypothesis and the relative income hypothesis. After criticising Keynes' and Duesenberry's theories, the life-cycle hypothesis by Modigliani and Brumberg and the permanent-income hypothesis of consumption by Friedman were suggested as 'sounder' approaches. Both of these formulations were based on Irving Fisher's theory of intertemporal choice with utility maximising and forward-looking agents. Intertemporal choice theory effectively excludes any sociological or psychological influences on consumption decisions. The chapter then focuses on the life-cycle and permanent-income hypotheses of consumption, also examining their main differences in terms of theory and policy implications.

After the emergence of life-cycle and permanent-income consumption hypotheses, the constrained utility-maximiser model of individual behaviour became the theoretical microeconomic basis of orthodox macroeconomics. Chapter 7 starts with a discussion of Robert Hall's random walk theory of consumption with rational expectations. It proceeds with the rise of the representative agent models (RANK), in which the consumption function usually consists of a representative agent maximising his/her utility over an infinite lifetime without borrowing constraints. The rise of

RANK formulations was almost parallel to the gradual emergence of the new neoclassical synthesis, also known as Dynamic Stochastic General Equilibrium (DSGE) theory. The chapter also considers the empirical testing of the random-walk theories and their modifications in view of their empirical shortcomings. Modern variations of the above models with reference to consumption function such as the Heterogeneous Agent New Keynesian (HANK) and the Two-Agents New Keynesian (TANK) models are also discussed.

Parallel to the formation of orthodox consumption functions, there were alternative approaches to aggregate consumption originating from non-mainstream authors and schools of thought. These approaches criticised the basic assumptions and the underlying methodological framework of mainstream consumption functions. Chapter 8 begins with a discussion of their views, starting with James Tobin whose work represents the standard Keynesian approach (sometimes labelled as 'Old Keynesian'). It continues with a presentation of Michael Kalecki and Kaleckian-based approaches, and with the views on consumption developed by Nicholas Kaldor and Luigi Pasinetti. Finally, it outlines the broad common characteristics concerning aggregate consumption found in the contemporary Post Keynesian school.

Chapter 9 presents the methodological setting in which contemporary aggregate consumption theories were developed. It also summarises the major criticisms that have been applied to this setting by various economists belonging to different intellectual traditions, including heterodox macroeconomists. The chapter begins with a brief overview of the main strands of contemporary mainstream macroeconomics. It then considers its three fundamental components: microfoundations, the role of the representative agent, and the unifying framework of methodological individualism. The chapter concludes with a summary of the above issues contained in heterodox macroeconomic thinking.

The purpose of the final chapter is to provide a synopsis of the material discussed in the previous chapters with particular emphasis on the economic policy implications of the various consumption functions. In opposition to Keynes' and Duesenberry's approaches, the life-cycle and permanent-income hypotheses offered the first theoretical justifications against the key role of fiscal policy in economic stabilisation. The case for non-activist economic policy was strengthened with the modern versions of consumption function based on Euler's equation. Chapter 10 starts with a summary of the policy implications emerging from the consumption formulations found in Keynes, Duesenberry, and Keynesianism. In the same vein, it proceeds with the mainstream theories based on rational forward-looking optimising agents. There is also a discussion of the policy implications emerging from Old or standard Keynesianism, Post Keynesian, heterodox consumption formulations, and non-mainstream strands such as the new behavioural economics. The presence of ideological considerations in policy recommendations will also be briefly discussed. A general conclusion summarising the main arguments of this book closes the chapter.

References

Barro, R. (1979). On the Determination of the Public Debt. *Journal of Political Economy, 87*(5, Part 1), 940–971.

Bunting, D. (1989). The Consumption Function 'Paradox'. *Journal of Post Keynesian Economics, 11*(3), 347–359.

Chao, H.-K. (2003). Milton Friedman and the Emergence of the Permanent Income Hypothesis. *History of Political Economy, 35*(1), 77–104.

Deaton, A. (1992). *Macroeconomics and Consumption.* Oxford University Press.

Deaton, A. (2005). Franco Modigliani and the Life-Cycle Theory of Consumption. *BNL Quarterly Review, LVIII*(233–234), 91–107.

Duesenberry, J. S. (1949). *Income, Saving and the Theory of Consumer Behaviour.* Harvard University Press.

Edwards, J. (2014). Consumer Power and Market Control: Exploring Consumer Behaviour in Affluent Contexts (1946–1980). *The European Journal of the History of Economic Thought, 21*(4), 699–723.

Eltis, A. (1980). Malthus's Theory of Effective Demand and Growth. *Oxford Economic Papers, 32*(1), 19–56.

Fiaschi, D., & Signorino, R. (2003). Consumption Patterns, Development and Growth: Adam Smith, David Ricardo and Thomas Robert Malthus. *European Journal of the History of Economic Thought, 10*(1), 5–24.

Fisher, I. (1930). *The Theory of Interest.* Macmillan.

Friedman, M. (1957). *The Consumption Function.* Princeton University Press.

Hall, R. E. (1978). Stochastic Implications of the Life Cycle-Permanent Income Hypothesis: Theory and Evidence. *Journal of Political Economy, 86*(6), 971–987.

Hynes, A. H. (1998). The Emergence of the Neoclassical Consumption Function: The Formative Years. 1940–1952. *Journal of the History of Economic Thought, 20*(01), 25–49.

Jappelli, T., & Pistaferri, L. (2017). *The Economics of Consumption: Theory and Evidence.* Oxford University Press.

Kaldor, N. (1955–1956). Alternative Theories of Distribution. *The Review of Economics Studies, 23*(2), 83–100.

Kalecki, M. (1971). *Selected Essays on the Dynamics of the Capitalist Economy*. Cambridge University Press.

Keynes, J. M. (1936). *The General Theory of Employment, Interest, and Money*. Macmillan.

Kuznets, S. (1942). *Uses of National Income in Peace and War*. National Bureau of Economic Research.

Kyrk, H. (1923). *Theory of Consumption*. Houghton Miffin.

Lucas, R. E. (1972). Expectations and the Neutrality of Money. *Journal of Economic Theory, 4*(2), 103–124.

Malthus, T. R. (1986). *The Works of Thomas Robert Malthus* (E.A. Wrigley and D. Souden, Ed.). William Pickering.

Mason, R. (2000). The Social Significance of Consumption: James Duesenberry's Contribution to Consumer Theory. *Journal of Economic Issues, 34*(3), 553–572.

Modigliani, F., & Brumberg, R. (1954). Utility Analysis and the Consumption Function: An Interpretation of Cross-Section Data. In K. K. Kurihara (Ed.), *Post-Keynesian Economics* (pp. 388–436). Rutgers University Press.

Muellbauer, J. (2016). Macroeconomics and Consumption, *Economics Series Working Papers Paper*, No. 811, University of Oxford, Department of Economics, Oxford, UK, pp.1–37.

Palley, T. (2010). Relative Permanent Income Theory of Consumption: A Synthetic Keynes- Duesenberry- Friedman model. *Review of Political Economy, 22*(1), 41–56.

Pasinetti, L. (1962). Rate of Profit and Income Distribution in Relation to the Rate of Economic Growth. *The Review of Economic Studies, 29*(4), 267–279.

Pignalosa, D. (2025). Consumption as a Social Phenomenon in the Modern Theory of Intertemporal Choice. *Review of Political Economy, 37*(2), 543–563.

Richmond, W. (1978). John A. Hobson: Economic Heretic. *The American Journal of Economics and Sociology, 37*(3), 283–294.

Rutherford, R. (1987). Malthus and Keynes. *Oxford Economic Papers, 39*(1), 175–189.

Stiglitz, J. (2018). Where Modern Macroeconomics Went Wrong. *Oxford Review of Economic Policy, 34*(1–2), 70–106.

Thomas, A. (2024). Classical Economics and the Question of Aggregate Demand. *Review of Political Economy* 36(3), 1064–1078

Thomas, A. (2025). Keynes and Ricardo on Consumption, *Cambridge Journal of Economics,* 49(5), 999–1014.

Tobin, J. (1951). Relative Income, Absolute Income, and Saving. Reprinted in *Essays in Economics, 2: Consumption and Econometrics*. MIT Press: Cambridge, 1987.

Todorova, Z. (2014). Consumption as a Social Process. *Journal of Economic Issues, 48*(3), 663–678.

Trezzini, A. (2012). Relative Consumption vs. Permanent Income: The Crisis of the Theory of the Social Significance of Consumption. *Journal of the History of Economic Thought, 34*(3), 355–377.

Trezzini, A. (2016). Early Contributions to the Economics of Consumption as a Social Phenomenon. *European Journal of the History of Economic Thought, 23*(2), 272–296.

Veblen, T. (1899a). The Preconceptions of Economic Science. *Quarterly Journal of Economics, 13*, 121–150.

Veblen, T. (1899b). *The Theory of the Leisure Class.* Macmillan.

Woodford, M. (2009). Convergence in Macroeconomics: Elements of the New Synthesis, *American Economic Journal: Macroeconomics, 1*(1): 267–279.

CHAPTER 2

Approaches to Consumption Before Keynes

Introduction

Before Keynes' systematic treatment of aggregate consumption expenditures and their role in the economy, there were a number of works which set the conceptual basis of the notion connecting it to its social dimension. For instance, Henry Cunynghame (1892) and Caroline Foley (1893) identified status-driven consumption as shaping the demand for many consumer goods, and pointed out the analytical consequences that considerations of social interdependencies in consumption may have for economic theory (see also Berry, 1994; Bianchi & Sanfilippo, 2015). However, the most influential was the work of Thorstein Veblen, and especially his *Theory of the Leisure Class* (1899), in which he discussed key economic concepts such as property, wealth, and consumption. Veblen was among the founders of the Institutional school with the American economists Wesley Mitchell and John Commons. Institutionalism was a distinct school of economic thought with considerable impact on the English-speaking world. Veblen's ideas on consumption were further developed by economists belonging to the Institutionalist tradition. Hazel Kyrk was a key figure of this tradition when it comes to the theory of consumption. At the same period, there were also similar works on consumption by women economists in the US. The fundamental characteristic of the Institutionalist approach to consumption was the emphasis on the social dimension of consumption.

S. A. Drakopoulos, *The Consumption Function in Economics*,
https://doi.org/10.1007/978-3-032-15958-8_2

This chapter will start with a discussion of Veblen's critique of Marginalism and of Neoclassical economics in general. It will proceed with Veblen's introduction and analysis of the notion of conspicuous consumption. The chapter will continue with the work of Hazel Kyrk on consumption and savings. It will also briefly present the views on consumption of women Institutionalist economists in the US.

Veblen: Critique of Marginalism and of Neoclassical Economics

Veblen attacked the hedonistic psychology underlying Marginalism and Neoclassical economics and suggested an analysis of instincts and habits as a substitute psychological foundation to psychological hedonism. In particular, after the rise of Marginalism, Veblen was the first major figure to focus his criticism to the established model of individual economic behaviour. The tone is set in one of his early papers where he clearly dismisses the narrow hedonistic conception of individual economic behaviour by mainstream economists of his time (the work of Alfred Marshall was one of his targets, see Mason, 1995, pp. 872–874). As he wrote:

> *The hedonistic conception of man is that of a lightning calculator of pleasures and pains, who oscillates like a homogeneous globule of desire of happiness under the impulse of stimuli that shift him about the area, but leave him intact. He has neither antecedent nor consequent. He is an isolated, definitive human datum, in stable equilibrium except for the buffets of the impinging forces that displace him in one direction or – another.* (Veblen, 1899a, p. 389)

Veblen attacked the hedonistic basis of orthodox economic theory arguing that it was incapable of taking into consideration the social influences on consumption decisions (Mason, 1995). He also criticised the orthodox tendency to reduce the rich institutional and cultural diversity of economic and social life to tidy, mechanical formal models (Dimand, 1998). Many orthodox theorists viewed the model of individual economic behaviour as an abstract construction, representing only one aspect of human nature (Drakopoulos, 2011). Veblen, nevertheless, did not submit to this dualism (fictional versus real individual, or economic versus non-economic) and condemned this conception on methodological grounds. In Veblen's words:

> *Of course, this perfect competitive system, with its untainted "economic man", is a feat of scientific imagination, and is not intended as a competent expression of fact. It is an expedient of abstract reasoning; and its avowed competency extends only to the abstract principles, the fundamental laws of science, which hold only in so far as the abstraction holds. But, as happens in such cases, having once been accepted and assimilated as real, though perhaps not as actual, it becomes an effective constituent in the inquirer's habits of thought and goes to shape his knowledge of facts.* (Veblen, 1899a, pp. 142–143)

By claiming that the entire structure of orthodox economic theory was based on hedonistic foundations, Veblen dismissed the standard approach to economic behaviour. The notion of economic man leaves out important elements of human behaviour, and thus it is characterised as very simplistic and unrealistic (Veblen, 1899a).[1] Veblen's critique of neoclassical economics reverberated in the economic thought of most subsequent institutional economists. For instance, Walton Hamilton wrote: "The extreme individualism, rationality, and utilitarianism which animated eighteenth century thought still finds expression in neo-classical economics" (Hamilton, 1919, p. 816).

Veblen proposed an entirely different psychology on which economics should be based. He argued that people are not motivated by rational, selfish, hedonistic considerations, but by a variety of instincts and habits. Instincts, which are always changing, and so human behaviour is always in evolution, play a key role in Veblen's economic thought (Goodwin, 2016, p. 96).[2] As examples of instincts, Veblen suggested the instinct of workmanship, the drive towards providing for the family and society (parental bent), and the drive to produce interpretations of the world (idle curiosity). The instinct of workmanship is the "more generic, more abiding trait of human nature", guided by this "proclivity for turning the material means of life to account" (Veblen, 1899b, p. 190). Moreover, he was keen to emphasise that habits of thought are the other key determinant of behaviour. In turn, habits of thought give birth to institutions. The interaction of instincts and habits of thought produce new institutions through

[1] Veblen's methodological critique of utility maximising individuals has also influenced contemporary institutional economists. An indicative example is G. Hodgson's work (e.g. Hodgson, 2000).

[2] Veblen's analysis of instincts can be mainly attributed to psychologist William James influence (Edgell & Tilman, 1989; Rutherford, 2001).

an evolutionary process (Veblen, 1914; see also Seckler, 1975; Rutherford, 1984; Papageorgiou et al., 2013).[3]

Veblen: Conspicuous Consumption

Given his previous attack on the dominant conception of economic behaviour as selfish, Veblen placed particular emphasis on the social aspects of human nature. In his *Theory of the Leisure Class* (1899b), Veblen discussed key economic concepts such as property, wealth, and consumption. His analysis of these concepts is based on the broad idea that individuals always engage in social comparisons. After connecting the motive of emulation to the institution of private property, the notions of social comparisons, social status, and social ranking are discussed:

> *the end sought by accumulation is to rank high in comparison with the rest of the community in point of pecuniary strength. So long as the comparison is distinctly unfavourable to himself, the normal, average individual will live in chronic dissatisfaction with his present lot; and when he has reached what may be called the normal pecuniary standard of the community, or of his class in the community, this chronic dissatisfaction will give place to a restless straining to place a wider and ever-widening pecuniary interval between himself and this average standard.* (Veblen, 1899b, pp. 31–32)

Furthermore, Veblen's famous term, *conspicuous consumption*, is vitally related to the above. According to Veblen, conspicuous consumption is the consumption of luxuries that is observed by others, sometimes by these others participating in it. Conspicuous consumption is not confined to the rich or to the *leisure class* in Veblen's terminology. Other social classes might also engage in such activity, even the lower classes. As he declared:

> *No class of society, not even the most abjectly poor, foregoes all customary conspicuous consumption. … There is no class and no country that has yielded so*

[3] Asso and Fiorito (2004, p. 449) elaborate: "Veblen's instincts, in fact, must be viewed in their dynamic relationship with the environment: on the one hand it is the influence exercised by the institutional framework on the hereditary make-up of individuals that determines human conduct; on the other it is the continuous search of ways and means to satisfy these hereditary tendencies that gives rise to habits, which in turn become incorporated into a body of culture and originate institutions, social conventions, and human enterprises."

abjectly before the pressure of physical want as to deny themselves all gratification of this higher or spiritual need. (Veblen, 1899b, p. 85)

Therefore to the Veblenian conspicuous consumer, the joy comes from the successful exhibition of status through material possessions.[4] Veblen believed that the acquisition of these status goods strongly influences the behaviour of the consumers, becoming the very impetus for their actions (Almeida, 2015). The lack of conspicuous consumption implies the loss of both social repute and self-respect (Veblen, 1899b, p. 111).[5] It follows that the demand for consumption goods derives mainly from their social significance rather than their intrinsic utility, something which is in opposition to the Marginalist approach. Given that all social classes engage in conspicuous consumption, aggregate consumption is then the sum of individual expenditures determined by the standards adopted by individual households (Trezzini, 2024).

The central role of social status implies that when the individuals' level of income drops, they seek to maintain the level of consumption to which they and their families are accustomed (Trezzini, 2016, p. 274). On the contrary and due to social emulation, when their income rises, individuals tend to increase their consumption by purchasing conspicuous goods that elevate their social status. Consumption behaviour is therefore asymmetrical with respect to changes in income (Trezzini, 2016, p. 274; also Veblen, 1899b, p. 103). The notion of the irreversibility of consumption expenditure, as it is known nowadays, played a crucial role in James Duesenberry's (1949) consumption theory. Although Veblen develops a detailed analysis of the determinants of consumption expenditure, he did not elaborate on the relationship between the determinants of consumption expenditure and those of savings (Trezzini, 2016, p. 275).

Veblen's approach to consumption influenced leading figures of American Institutionalism such as Wesley Mitchell (1912), and also of prominent sociologists such as William Ogburn (1923). Mitchell argued that "spending money" was a "backward art". In his view, consumption decisions tend to be taken with reference to socially determined standards

[4] Jon Wisman argues convincingly that both Adam Smith and Veblen saw humans as seeking self-respect by acquiring approval or social certification from others, often pursued through conspicuous consumption (Wisman, 2019).

[5] It has been maintained that there is relative agreement among Smith, Rae, Mill, Veblen, and Keynes that this type of consumption has socially deleterious effects (Camatta & Salles, 2025).

rather than being the result of rational choices. Similarly, Ogburn assumed consumption as socially determined with an average composition of consumption baskets that changes according to the relative position of the consumer unit on the social ladder (Trezzini, 2016, p. 276). In a similar vein to Veblen, he argued that even "workers' families will go without the necessary food, clothing, and warmth in order to get recreation or purchase services or goods that have to do with social standing" (Ogburn, 1923, p. 21).[6] John Commons, the other major figure of 'old institutionalism', also accepted the notion of consumption irreversibility and proceeded to a discussion of its effects. More specifically, in a context where decisions are irreversible and uncertainty matters, the liquidity preference shapes the behaviour of economic agents (Tymoigne, 2003; Ferrari-Filho & Conceição, 2005). It should be noted that Commons' reasoning exhibited some common points with Keynes' arguments on the non-neutrality of money and on uncertainty.[7]

The initial reception of the *Theory of the Leisure Class* was rather negative (Dorfman, 1934; Dolfsma, 2000). Veblen's consumption analysis was completely at odds with the neoclassical economists of the period. As a result, his observations were marginalised from mainstream economics (Dobriansky, 1957). Nevertheless, Veblen's insights have influenced a number of subsequent approaches to consumption patterns analysis (see also Chap. 7). For instance, the idea of following behaviour or keeping up with the Joneses has appeared in a number of modern formulations including aggregate consumption such as in Galí, 1994; Clark & Oswald, 1998; Ljungqvist & Uhlig, 2000; Ulph, 2014 (for a review, see Pignalosa, 2025). Veblen's analysis on consumption was also a major influence to J. K. Galbraith who attacked the orthodox economic assumptions of consumer demand by highlighting the nature of conspicuous economic display (Galbraith, 1958; see also Chirat, 2020). Further, works by some modern institutionalist and heterodox economists have built on Veblen's views on consumption (e.g. Hamilton, 1987; Todorova, 2014).

[6] It has been argued that Ogburn's work can be seen as the first empirical estimate of a "Keynesian" saving function years before the *General Theory* (Thomas, 1989).

[7] Keynes corresponded with Commons about economic policy. In 1927, Keynes wrote: "There seems to me to be no other economist with whose general way of thinking I feel myself in such genuine accord" (Atkinson & Oleson, 1998, p. 1019; see also Whalen, 2020).

Hazel Kyrk's Theory of Consumption and Savings

It has been recognised that Hazel Kyrk's *A Theory of Consumption* (1923) was a key contribution to consumption economics of the period (Dorfman, 1959; Rutherford, 2011; see also the papers in 100 years after the publication of *A Theory of Consumption* by Hazel Kyrk, symposium published in 2023).[8] Kyrk's work was basically an institutionalist analysis that built on the works of Veblen and Mitchell (Todorova, 2024). The starting point of Kyrk's approach was that consumption is a social phenomenon influenced by social factors such as social class, social norms, and the desire for social status.[9] As a first observation, one can notice her conception of consumers as characterised by complex behaviour. As she argued:

> *Individuals as consumers are not blocks of stone or lumps of clay, but complexities of propensities, interests and purposes, wise and foolish, acquired and innate, the result of suggestions which have come to them from many sources.* (Kyrk, 1923, p. 105)

Regarding the issue of the complexity of humans, and particularly the explanation of how consumption standards change, Kyrk followed some of Veblen's conceptualisations of "instincts" or proclivities that he identified as regularities in different forms throughout human history (Todorova, 2024, p. 35). Consequently, she emphasised the social nature of individual preferences:

> *The social nature of our scales of preference or standards of living is shown most clearly by the attitude of the individual toward them.* (Kyrk, 1923, p. 179)

Further, Veblen's basic ideas concerning the determination of consumption expenditures can be found in her main work. Consumption decisions are based on socially determined standards generally associated with a particular group or social class (Kyrk, 1923, p. 172). Following Veblen, Kyrk assigned the respect of their neighbours and self-esteem as powerful drives of consumers decisions. In particular, failure to keep up with a social standard of consumption leads to feelings of inadequacy and

[8] Research in the History of Economic Thought and Methodology: Including a Symposium on Hazel Kyrk's A Theory of Consumption 100 Years after Publication, 2023, Volume 41D.

[9] For a history of the economics of consumption and its links to home economics in the US, see Philippy (2021).

inferiority, which are severely detrimental to self-esteem (Trezzini, 2016, p. 280). In her own words:

> *The strength of standards of living over the individual is well shown in the resistance that he offers to a threatened lowering of his consumption below the standard.* (Kyrk, 1923, p. 181)

The asymmetry of consumption expenditure with respect to changes in income is also present in Kyrk's work. She argued that as income increases, individuals tend to expand their consumption to maintain or improve their social standing. Conversely, when income falls, consumers strive to maintain their consumption standards to avoid losing social standing. More precisely:

> *Yet it is believed that the resistance to pressure downward is stronger than the effort to move upward. The individual will not exert himself as much to improve his mode of living above the standard as he will struggle to maintain it; he will not feel privation and dissatisfaction to the same extent if he is unable to live above his standard as if he had fallen below.* (Kyrk, 1923, pp. 184–185)

Kyrk engaged in a more detailed discussion of savings patterns than Veblen. She identified three distinct categories of savings. The first category has to do with the acquisition of consumers' goods which call for relatively heavy expenditure. From the individual standpoint and while they are being accumulated, these savings serve as capital (Kyrk, 1923, p. 271). Saving for the provision of future needs is another category of savings (one might identify it with precautionary savings). Providing for the future can be regarded as essential to self-esteem and retaining the respect of others (Kyrk, 1923, p. 272; see also Trezzini, 2016). Finally, there is a third type of saving that can clearly be viewed as residual.

> [*This] is what has been called automatic or costless savings. It is unplanned saving with no particular purpose in view, saving which takes place when surplus is so large that individual reaches his practical spending limit upon both essential and luxuries before it is used up. The remainder of the income will be automatically saved.* (Kyrk, 1923, p. 272)

The type of savings that she describes can be conceived as the origin of the elasticity of aggregate saving with respect to income that is higher during recessions than during expansions. Aggregate saving is thus made up of different parts, some of which clearly display a residual nature and asymmetrical behaviour. The whole amount of saving would therefore present inverse asymmetrical behaviour with respect to that of consumption (Trezzini, 2016, pp. 282–283). In her subsequent work, Kyrk focused on the quantitative foundations of consumption including a statistical analysis of variations of family expenditures (e.g. Kyrk, 1937; Alberti & Asso, 2025). At the time of its publication, Kyrk's theory was well received but its overall academic impact was rather limited (Philippy et al., 2024).

Apart from Kyrk, Veblen's views on consumption were also developed by a group of women economists in the US who were inspired by the Institutionalist tradition. Theresa Schmid McMahon, Elizabeth Waterman Gilboy, and Jessica Blanche Peixotto were the main figures. McMahon focused on the evolution of living standards in the framework of economic and institutional changes. Consequently, she examined the macroeconomic implications of social influences on consumption. Adopting the standard assumption that growth is driven by savings, she argued that 'conspicuous consumption' has negative effects on economic growth (McMahon, 1925). According to Gilboy, the process of consumption emulation implies that new goods (initially perceived as luxuries) are gradually incorporated into the acquired standard of living which tends to raise the consumption standards of the whole economy (Gilboy, 1932). It is also interesting that in her subsequent work, she viewed Keynes' psychological law of consumption as a basic law of human nature driving individual behaviour (Gilboy, 1938, p. 140; see also O'Donnell, 2018).[10] Finally, Peixotto's work has been described as an outline of relative-income theory of consumption much before Duesenberry's well-known formulation (Peixotto, 1927; Thomas, 1989, p. 135). The basic and common point of the works of the group was their approach to consumption as a social phenomenon (for a detailed discussion, see Trezzini, 2024).

Concluding Comments

Veblen's work represents the first systematic attempt to analyse consumption decisions and patterns. After attacking the Marginalist modelling of consumption decisions, the core of his discussion was the notion of the social relevance of consumption. Veblen's approach initiated a tradition

[10] Gilboy and Keynes had an exchange of views regarding Keynes' psychological law of consumption (see O'Donnell, 2018).

among mainly American Institutional economists who studied the social aspects of consumption and savings. The most prominent of those economists was the work of Kyrk in which she elaborated and extended Veblen's ideas on consumption and saving. The works of McMahon, Gilboy, and Peixotto were also in the same conceptual framework. Thus, in the first decades of the twentieth century, there was a body of knowledge that viewed and analysed consumption patterns mainly as a social phenomenon.

The next major step on aggregate consumption analysis can be found in J. M Keynes consumption theory where the social dimension of consumption and saving decisions was also present. It is not certain how much Keynes was influenced by the Institutionalist's contributions (for arguments supporting Keynes's knowledge of Institutionalism, see Trezzini, 2024). Nevertheless, there are important common points such as Keynes' use of Veblen's classification of needs as 'absolute' and 'relative', and the conception of saving as a residual, found in Kyrk. The following chapter will turn to an examination of Keynes' consumption theory with special attention to its social dimension.

References

Alberti, M., & Asso, P. F. (2025). Hazel Kyrk and the Rise of Empirical Research in Interwar America. *Journal of the History of Economic Thought, 47*(2), 164–186.

Almeida, F. (2015). The Psychology of Early Institutional Economics: The Instinctive Approach of Thorstein Veblen's Conspicuous Consumer Theory. *OEconomia, 16*, 226–234.

Asso, P. F., & Fiorito, L. (2004). Human Nature and Economic Institutions: Instinct Psychology, Behaviorism, and the Development of American Institutionalism. *Journal of the History of Economic Thought, 26*, 445–477.

Atkinson, G., & Oleson, T. (1998). Commons and Keynes: Their Assault on Laissez Faire. *Journal of Economic Issues, 32*, 1019–1030.

Berry, C. (1994). *The Idea of Luxury: A Conceptual and Historical Investigation*. Cambridge University Press.

Bianchi, M., & Sanfilippo, E. (2015). Social Interdependencies in Consumption: An Early Economic Debate on Social Distinction, Emulation, and Fashion. *History of Political Economy, 47*(4), 547–575.

Camatta, R. B., & Salles, A. O. T. (2025). Motives, consequences and taxation of conspicuous consumption: Classics, Veblen, and Keynes. *Journal of Post Keynesian Economics, 48*(3), 521–541

Chirat, A. (2020). A Reappraisal of Galbraith's Challenge to Consumer Sovereignty: Preferences, Welfare and the Non-neutrality Thesis. *The European Journal of the History of Economic Thought, 27*(2), 248–275.

Clark, A., & Oswald, A. (1998). Comparison-Concave utility and Following Behaviour in Social and Economic Settings. *Journal of Public Economics, 70*, 133–155.

Cunynghame, H. (1892). Some Improvements in Simple Geometrical Methods of Treating Exchange Value, Monopoly, and Rent. *Economic Journal, 2*(5), 35–52.

Dimand, R. (1998). Fisher and Veblen: Two Paths for American Economics. *Journal of the History of Economic Thought, 20*(4), 449–465.

Dobriansky, L. (1957). *Veblenism: A New Critique*. Public Affairs Press.

Dolfsma, W. (2000). Life and Times of the Veblen Effect. *History of Economic Ideas, 8*(3), 61–82.

Dorfman, J. (1934). *Thorstein Veblen and his America*. The Viking Press.

Dorfman, J. (1959). *The Economic Mind in American Civilization* (Vol. IV and V). The Viking Press.

Drakopoulos, S. (2011). Wicksteed, Robbins and the Emergence of Mainstream Economic Methodology. *Review of Political Economy, 23*, 461–470.

Duesenberry, J. S. (1949). *Income, Saving and the Theory of Consumer Behaviour*. Harvard University Press.

Edgell, S., & Tilman, R. (1989). The Intellectual Antecedents of Thorstein Veblen: A Reappraisal. *Journal of Economic Issues, 23*, 1003–1026.

Ferrari-Filho, F., & Conceição, O. (2005). The Concept of Uncertainty in Post Keynesian Theory and in Institutional Economics. *Journal of Economic Issues, 39*(3), 579–594.

Foley, C. (1893). Fashion. *Economic Journal, 3*(11), 458–474.

Galbraith, J. K. (1958). *The Affluent Society*. Houghton Mifflin.

Galí, J. (1994). Keeping up with the Joneses: Consumption Externalities, Portfolio Choice, and Asset Prices. *Journal of Money, Credit and Banking, 26*(1), 1–8.

Gilboy, E. W. (1932). Demand as a Factor in the Industrial Revolution. In H. C. Arthur, A. L. Dunham, & N. S. B. Gras (Eds.), *Facts and Factors in Economic History. Articles by Former Students of Edwin Francis Gay* (pp. 620–639). Harvard University Press.

Gilboy, E. W. (1938). The Propensity to Consume. *Quarterly Journal of Economics, 53*(1), 120–140.

Goodwin, C. (2016). Economics and Psychology: Why the Great Divide? *History of Political Economy, 48*(suppl. 1), 71–169.

Hamilton, D. (1987). Institutional Economics and Consumption. *Journal of Economic Issues, 21*(4), 1531–1554.

Hamilton, W. (1919). The Institutional Approach to Economic Theory. *The American Economic Review, 9*(1), 309–318.

Hodgson, G. (2000). What is the Essence of Institutional Economics? *Journal of Economic Issues, 34*(2), 317–329.

Kyrk, H. (1923). *Theory of Consumption*. Houghton Miffin.

Kyrk, H. (1937). Methods of Measuring Variations in Family Expenditures: Discussion. *Journal of the American Statistical Association, 197*(3), 47–49.

Ljungqvist, L., & Uhlig, H. (2000). Tax Policy and Aggregate Demand Management Under Catching up with the Joneses. *American Economic Review, 90*(3), 356–366.

Mason, R. (1995). Interpersonal Effects on Consumer Demand in Economic Theory and Marketing Thought, 1890–1950. *Journal of Economic Issues, 29*, 871–881.

McMahon, T. (1925). *Social and Economic Standards of Living*. D.C. Heath.

Mitchell, W. (1912). The Backward Art of Spending Money. *The American Economic Review, 2*, 269–281.

O'Donnell, R. (2018). Clarifying Keynes's Theory of Consumption and Psychological Law. *History of Economics Review, 71*(1), 94–117.

Ogburn, W. (1923). The Standard of Living Factor in Wages. *The American Economic Review, 13*(Supplement 1), 118–128.

Papageorgiou, T., Katselidis, I., & Michaelides, P. (2013). Schumpeter, Commons, and Veblen on Institutions. *American Journal of Economics and Sociology, 72*(5), 1232–1254.

Peixotto, J. B. (1927). *Getting and Spending at the Professional Standard of Living: A Study of the Costs of an Academic Life*. Macmillan.

Philippy, D. (2021). Ellen Richards's Home Economics Movement and the Birth of the Economics of Consumption. *Journal of the History of Economic Thought, 43*(3), 378–400.

Philippy, D., Betancourt, R., & Dimand, R. (2024). Hazel Kyrk's Intellectual Roots: When First-generation Home Economists Met the Institutionalist Framework. *Research in the History of Economic Thought and Methodology, 41D*, 7–26.

Pignalosa, D. (2025). Consumption as a Social Phenomenon in the Modern Theory of Intertemporal Choice. *Review of Political Economy, 37*(2), 543–563.

Rutherford, M. (1984). Thorstein Veblen and the processes of institutional change. *History of Political Economy, 16*, 331–348.

Rutherford, M. (2001). Institutional Economics: Then and Now. *The Journal of Economic Perspectives, 15*, 173–194.

Rutherford, M. (2011). *The institutionalist Movement in American Economics, 1918–1947: Science and Social Control*. Cambridge University Press.

Seckler, D. (1975). *Thorstein Veblen and the Institutionalists*. Macmillan.

Thomas, J. J. (1989). The Early Econometric History of the Consumption Function. *Oxford Economic Papers, 41*(1), 131–149.

Todorova, Z. (2014). Consumption as a Social Process. *Journal of Economic Issues, 48*(3), 663–678.

Todorova, Z. (2024). Hazel Kyrk's A Theory of Consumption, Veblen's Business and Industrial Concerns, and W.C. Mitchell's Essays on Spending and Money: Conceptual Links. *Research in the History of Economic Thought and Methodology, 41D*, 27–45.

Trezzini, A. (2016). Early Contributions to the Economics of Consumption as a Social Phenomenon. *The European Journal of the History of Economic Thought, 23*(2), 272–296.

Trezzini, A. (2024). Hazel Kyrk, The Economics of the Social Relevance of Consumption and John Maynard Keynes' Consumption Function. *Research in the History of Economic Thought and Methodology, 41D*, 67–91.

Tymoigne, E. (2003). Keynes and Commons on Money. *Journal of Economic Issues, 37*(3), 527–545.

Ulph, D. (2014). Keeping up with the Joneses: Who Loses Out? *Economics Letters, 125*, 400–403.

Veblen, T. (1899a). The Preconceptions of Economic Science. *Quarterly Journal of Economics, 13*, 121–150.

Veblen, T. (1899b). *The Theory of the Leisure Class.* Macmillan.

Veblen, T. (1914). *The Instinct of Workmanship and the State of the Industrial Arts.* W. B. Huebsch.

Whalen, C. (2020). Post-Keynesian institutionalism: Past, Present, and Future. *Evolutionary and Institutional Economics Review, 17*, 71–92.

Wisman, J. (2019). Adam Smith and Thorstein Veblen on the Pursuit of Status Through Consumption Versus Work. *Cambridge Journal of Economics, 43*(1), 17–36.

CHAPTER 3

Aggregate Consumption in the Economics of John Maynard Keynes

Introduction

Keynes' contribution to the study of consumption was a vital part of his overall economic analysis. The Keynesian consumption function became a basic component of subsequent Keynesian-based macroeconomic thought, and Keynes' consumption theory was dominant for many decades after its first appearance. In Keynes' system, consumption depends on current income, and the marginal propensity to consume out of income determines the value of the multiplier. The assumptions about consumption by Keynes are the first step towards the construction of what became known as the Keynesian multiplier (for a historical account of the concept, see Wright, 1956). The value of the multiplier is crucial for the role of fiscal policy in economic stabilisation, especially during recessions. Further, Keynes' approach to aggregate consumption is largely 'psychological', and contrary to subsequent mainstream consumption theories, it is not based on the standard model of individual rational behaviour.

In order to acquire a better understanding of Keynes' consumption analysis, a discussion of his critique of orthodox formulations of consumption decisions is necessary. This chapter will start with Keynes' serious reservations regarding the standard model of decision making suggested by his contemporary orthodoxy. It will proceed with a presentation of Keynes' approach to consumption which also acknowledges the social relevance of consumption decisions. Finally, the standard Keynesian analysis

S. A. Drakopoulos, *The Consumption Function in Economics*,
https://doi.org/10.1007/978-3-032-15958-8_3

of aggregate consumption and its significance for the level of total output, employment, and the effects of economic policy will be examined.

Keynes' Criticism of Utility Theory

Modern mainstream consumption theories are grounded on the assumption of individual economic rationality.[1] The first formulations of this model are to be found in Marginalists and early Neoclassicals and especially in the works of W. S. Jevons, F. Y. Edgeworth, and I. Fisher. The philosophy of Bentham's utilitarianism/hedonism is the conceptual basis of the model of economic rationality (Lewin, 1996). In particular and as Veblen emphasised, the "hedonic calculus" approach of Marginalists and early Neoclassicals was openly connected to psychological hedonism (Bruni & Sugden, 2007; Goodwin, 2016). Thus, it is important to highlight Keynes' strong objections to Benthamite hedonism.[2] There are a number of places in Keynes' work where he explicitly attacks Bentham, the psychology and the philosophy of hedonism, and the Benthamite calculus of pleasure and pain in general (Drakopoulos, 1992). For instance:

> *How disappointing are the fruits, now that we have them, of the bright idea of reducing Economics to a mathematical application of the hedonistic calculus of Bentham.* (Keynes, 1933: 184n; see also 1937, pp. 213–214)

Keynes also attacks Edgeworth for not having considered "how far the initial assumptions of the marginal theory stand or fall with the utilitarian ethics and the utilitarian psychology" (Keynes, 1933, p. 260).[3] In the same framework, Keynes criticises the orthodox treatment of expectations. In an article published in 1937, Keynes gives a brief summary of the works of Ricardo, Marshall, Edgeworth, and Pigou in relation to their theories of long-run equilibrium. Keynes observed that those writers assumed expectations to be given "in a definite and calculable form", and also that

[1] In order to avoid confusion, the term *mainstream economics* is used here to include the Neoclassical synthesis, Monetarism, and New Classical macroeconomics. This is not an unusual practice (e.g. Galbacs, 2015).

[2] Keynes' philosophical influences was a significant factor of his attack on utilitarianism (for a discussion, see O'Donnell, 1989; Davis, 2009).

[3] F. Y. Edgeworth, a contemporary of Marshall, formulated a formal model of individual behaviour that was explicitly based on psychological hedonism (Edgeworth, 1881; see also Drakopoulos & Katselidis, 2015).

"risks were assumed to be capable of an exact actuarial computation" (Keynes, 1937, pp. 212–213). Further, he was openly against the reduction of "uncertainty to the same calculable status as that of certainty itself; just as in the Benthamite calculus of pains and pleasures" (Keynes, 1937, p. 213).

Keynes' revolutionary conception of probability and uncertainty is another important point which puts him at odds with what nowadays is termed expected utility theory. In his view, a probability concept based on frequency is "a wrong philosophical interpretation of probability" (Keynes, 1921, p. 342). For Keynes, probabilities are either numerically indeterminate or undefinable (Keynes, 1921, pp. 8–9; see also Lawson, 1988, pp. 42–44). This is in sharp contrast with the subsequent mainstream expected utility approach which views probability as based on frequency and as numerically measurable (e.g. Savage, 1962; Radner, 1968). Consequently, his conception of uncertainty corresponds to a situation of numerically immeasurable probability. Keynes' conception of uncertainty has been subsequently termed *fundamental uncertainty* (e.g. Carabelli, 1988). For Keynes, uncertainty cannot be reduced, mainly because a numerical probability distribution is not known (events are not replicable).[4] Keynesian uncertainty is therefore radically different from the reducible and calculable uncertainty that is used in the expected utility model.[5] The critique towards the expected utility approach continued in the *General Theory*:

> *[It is a] characteristic of human nature that a large proportion of our purposive activities depend on spontaneous optimism rather than on mathematical expectation, whether moral or hedonistic or economic.* (Keynes, 1936, p. 161)

In place of utility maximisation, Keynes assigned extreme importance to psychological processes, which have nothing to do with economic calculus. Sociological and especially psychological considerations play an epistemological role in Keynes' analysis (see Dow & Hillard, 1995). The term *animal spirits* is employed by Keynes to describe these psychological

[4] Many authors have emphasized Keynes' conception of uncertainty and its crucial role in his economic thought. Indicative works are: Minsky (1975), Lawson (1988), Lavoie (1994), Ferrari-Filho and Conceição (2005), Roncaglia (2009), Dow (2012).

[5] For a detailed analysis of Keynes' notion of fundamental uncertainty and its relation to individual behaviour, see Arena and Nasica (2021).

processes (Keynes, 1936, pp. 161–162; see also Dow & Dow, 2012).[6] In an indicative statement, he argued that:

> *[m]ost, probably, of our decisions to do something positive, the full consequences of which will be drawn out over many days to come, can only be taken as a result of animal spirits – of a spontaneous urge to action rather than inaction, and not as the outcome of a weighted average of quantitative benefits multiplied by quantitative probabilities.* (Keynes, 1936, pp. 161–162)

Finally, another reason for the rejection of the expected utility model as a microeconomic basis for macroeconomic analysis was Keynes' concern for the fallacy of composition. Keynes thought that there is "a vital difference between the theory of the economic behaviour of the aggregate and the theory of the behaviour of the individual unit" (Keynes, 1936, p. 85). Keynes' frequent use of the term 'the community as a whole' clearly indicates that he was well aware of this important methodological notion (see also Chick & Jespersen, 2023).[7]

Consumption in Keynes' Economic Thought

Keynes' serious reservations concerning the utility maximising model led him to a formulation of consumption patterns which had nothing to do with intertemporal utility maximisation analysis. In Keynes' thought, actions and decisions of both consumers and producers are subject to fundamental uncertainty, and therefore they tend to follow some conventional rules (D'Orlando & Sanfilippo, 2010). More specifically, he argued that consumption depends on a) objective and b) subjective factors and states the following subjective factors which he calls motives: Enjoyment, Short-sightedness, Generosity, Miscalculation, Ostentation, and Extravagance. The corresponding list for savings behaviour is as follows: Precaution, Foresight, Calculation, Improvement, Independence, Enterprise, Pride, and Avarice (Keynes, 1936, p. 108). Keynes gives equal weight to these motives, something which is incompatible with the utility maximising model. He also placed great emphasis on the importance of habits at least in the short run (Keynes, 1936, p. 97).

[6] In the last two decades, the notion of animal spirits has regained popularity even among non-heterodox economists (e.g. Akerlof & Shiller, 2009).

[7] The fallacy of composition is closely connected to the issue of microfoundations which will be discussed in Chap. 9.

Further, in Keynes' framework the failure of money wages to fall in times of massive unemployment can be understood by reference to the highly rigid structure of wage differentials. Workers resist a cut in money wages in order to maintain their relative position in the wage structure and not so much to avoid a cut in their absolute income. In his words: "The effect of combination on the part of a group of workers is to protect their *relative* real wage" (Keynes, 1936, p. 14, original italics). In general, Keynes approached the consumption decision from an entirely different angle than mainstream economists before him. His approach was essentially a psychological approach emphasising also the sociological dimension of consumption patterns (Drakopoulos, 1992; D'Orlando & Sanfilippo, 2010).

The nature of consumption decisions was an important component of Keynes' system and a substantial point of difference from the classical line of thought. For most economists before Keynes, the economy was always naturally tending towards full-employment equilibrium, and this means that the short run income does not vary since its level is established at its full-employment level (see also Keynes, 1937). Given constant income, variations in consumption and saving depend on the rate of interest. This is the basic argument in Fisher's analysis of the interest rate as the major determinant of the allocation of income between intertemporal consumption and savings (Fisher, 1930). By rejecting the idea that the economy tends towards full employment, Keynes pointed out the differences between the actual level of income and the full-employment level. In Keynes' view, the level of aggregate demand determines equilibrium income, and since consumption is a major part of aggregate demand, it was necessary to provide a theory of the behaviour of consumption expenditures.

Although Keynes did not deny the relevance of the interest rate for consumption decisions as suggested by the orthodoxy, he downplayed it considerably (Keynes, 1937). In the *General Theory*, current income is the main determinant of consumption expenditures (absolute income hypothesis). In the Keynesian consumption function, the marginal propensity to consume is positive but less than one, and the average propensity to consume falls as income rises. In Keynes' words:

> *The fundamental psychological law, upon which we are entitled to depend with great confidence both a priori and from our knowledge of human nature and from the detailed facts of experience, is that men are disposed, as a rule and on*

> *the average, to increase their consumption, as their income increases, but not by as much as the increase in their income.* (Keynes, 1936, p. 96)

In general, Keynes' consumption analysis contains substantial psychological and sociological dimensions. For instance, when individuals face fundamental uncertainty, they tend to follow the social norms or the "rest of the world". As he wrote:

> *Knowing that our own individual judgment is worthless, we endeavor to fall back on the judgment of the rest of the world which is perhaps better informed.* (Keynes, 1936, p. 152)

Keynes was also especially sympathetic to the reality of status-driven consumption (see Mason, 1995, p. 877). Further, it is indicative that in his subsequent article (Keynes, 1937), he emphasised that "the psychological law underlying the Multiplier has escaped notice" (Keynes, 1937, p. 223). Overall, Keynes offered a rich, moderately complicated theory of consumption encompassing dynamics and statics, generality, and openness to varying historical conditions (see also O'Donnell, 2018).

The Standard Keynesian Consumption Function Analysis

Keynes' major work was extremely influential in the decades after its publication (Skidelsky, 1996). There were, and still are, many interpretations of his *General Theory*, and the relevant literature is enormous and still growing. The standard interpretation of Keynes' approach to consumption is much less open to debate, and the Keynesian-based formulations of the consumption function can be found in many subsequent texts (e.g. Snowdon & Vane, 2005; see also Pignalosa, 2021). From his analysis of the consumption function, Keynes developed the concept of the marginal propensity to consume, which plays a crucial role in the determination of the size of the government spending, investment, and tax multipliers (for a discussion, see Dimand, 1988).

Starting with Keynes' absolute income hypothesis (AIH), the Keynesian consumption function is usually written in a linear form:

$$C = \alpha + bY \tag{3.1}$$

In Eqn. (3.1), *C* is consumption expenditures, *Y* is current income, α is consumption expenditures that are independent of income (or autonomous consumption), and *b* is the marginal propensity to consume (MPC) or the ratio of the change in consumer spending to a change in income. The MPC is also the slope of the consumption function as Eqn. (3.2) shows.

$$MPC = \frac{\partial C}{\partial Y} = b \tag{3.2}$$

The average propensity to consume (APC), which is the ratio of total consumption to total income, is also given in Eqn. (3.3) as:

$$APC = \frac{C}{Y} = \frac{a}{Y} + b \tag{3.3}$$

The Keynesian consumption function can be presented with a simple diagram as Fig. 3.1 shows.

In Fig. 3.1, consumption expenditures (*C*) are represented on the vertical axis while income (*Y*) is on the horizontal axis. All the points of the 45°degree line show equality between consumption and income.

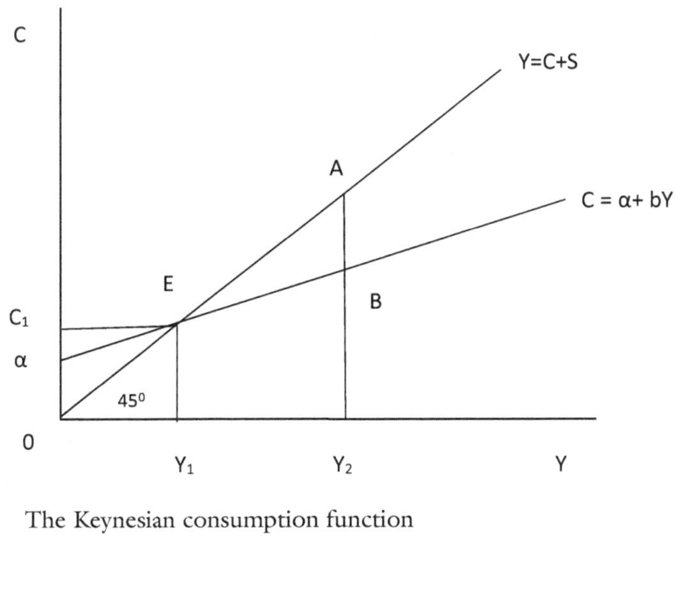

Fig. 3.1 The Keynesian consumption function

Consumption starts at point α with slope b. At equilibrium point E, all income is spent on consumption ($Y = C$), and savings are zero. For income levels lower than Y_1, consumption expenditures are higher than income and therefore savings are negative (borrowing). For income levels higher than Y_1, consumption expenditures are lower than income and therefore savings are positive. For instance, for a high level of income Y_2, consumption is lower than income and savings are equal to the distance given by AB.

As was seen before, Keynes thought that the MPC is positive but less than one, and that the APC falls as income rises. This implies that households with higher income will consume more (given that MPC > 0), will save more (given that MPC < 1), and that APC will be falling as income increases. How the APC varies as income changes depend on autonomous consumption (α). In the normal case ($a > 0$), MPC < APC and households spend a decreasing share of their incomes as incomes rise. If $a = 0$, MPC = APC and spending is a constant proportion b of income. These become clearer if we note that:

$$MPC = \frac{\partial C}{\partial Y} = b \, and \, APC = \frac{C}{Y} = \frac{a}{Y} + b \tag{3.4}$$

In order to see the multiplier effect of a change in autonomous consumption, we assume a very simple macroeconomic closed economy model with no government expenditure. National income (Y) comprises of consumption expenditures (C) and private autonomous investment (I_0). The equilibrium level of income Y^* is given by Eqn. (3.5):

$$Y^* = \frac{1}{1-b}\left(a + I_0\right) \tag{3.5}$$

The effect of a change in autonomous consumption on the equilibrium level of income is given in Eqn. (3.6) as:

$$\frac{dY^*}{da} = \frac{1}{1-b} > 0 \tag{3.6}$$

The case of an increase in autonomous consumption on the equilibrium level of income can also be illustrated by the following Fig. 3.2:

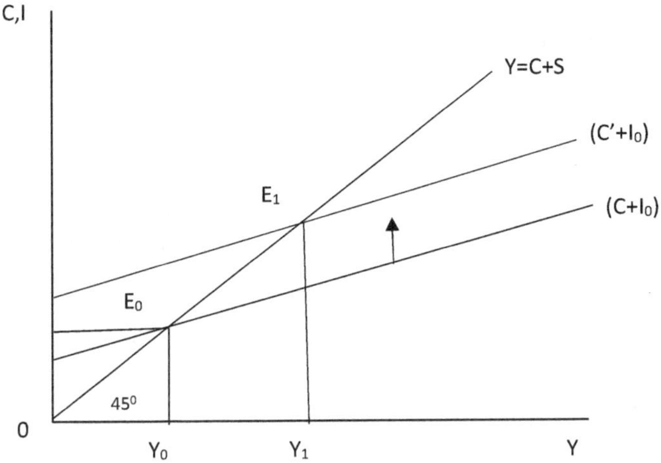

Fig. 3.2 The multiplier effect of a change in autonomous consumption

In Fig. 3.2, consumption expenditures (C) and private investment expenditures (I) are represented on the vertical axis, while income (Y) is on the horizontal axis. An increase in autonomous consumption from C to C' implies a shift of consumption function upwards from $C + I_0$ to $C' + I_0$, and a change of equilibrium from E_0 to E_1. The equilibrium level of income increases from Y_0 to Y_1. Due to the multiplier effect, the increase in Y is larger than the increase in autonomous consumption.

The economic policy implications of Keynes' approach are well known (see, for instance, Skidelsky, 1992; Dow, 2023).[8] The magnitude of the MPC determines the magnitude of the Keynesian multiplier and thus the effectiveness of fiscal policy to maintain or restore full employment.[9] As an illustration and assuming a simple closed economy macroeconomic model with government expenditures, we have $Y = C + I + G$. National income

[8] For an interesting interpretation of Keynes' long-term vision of economic policy and of capitalism, see Komine (2023).

[9] The terms of Keynesian multiplier and fiscal multipliers are often used interchangeably but they are not identical notions. Although government, tax, and fiscal multipliers can be explained with reference to the Keynesian multiplier, they measure empirically estimated effects on income that occur in different periods following a fiscal shock. The Keynesian multiplier measures a theoretical, simultaneous, total effect of any autonomous expenditure (Drakopoulos, 2021).

(Y) comprises of consumption expenditures (C), private investment (I), and government expenditures (G). A very simple tax system is assumed given as $T = T_0$. The equilibrium level of income (Y^*) is given by:

$$Y^* = \frac{1}{1-b}\left(a + I_0 + \mathrm{G0} - b\mathrm{T0}\right) \tag{3.7}$$

In Eqn. (3.7), I_0, G_0, and T_0 are autonomous private investment, autonomous government expenditure, and autonomous taxes, respectively. The ratio of the change in income to a change of investment is called the investment multiplier (m). In the simple Keynesian model, the private investment multiplier is given by Eqn. (3.8):

$$\frac{dY*}{dI} = \frac{1}{1-b} > 0 \tag{3.8}$$

Similarly, the government expenditure and the tax multipliers are:

$$\frac{dY*}{dG} = \frac{1}{1-b} > 0 \tag{3.9}$$

$$\frac{dY*}{dT} = \frac{-b}{1-b} < 0 \tag{3.10}$$

Equations (3.9) and (3.10) indicate that the larger the MPC, the larger the multiplier. They also show that the government expenditure multiplier is stronger than the tax multiplier. The MPC also implies that as households spend a decreasing share of their incomes as society becomes richer (at the margin), a greater proportion of investment will be required to maintain full-employment income levels. In addition and given that MPC < APC, a transfer of income from high-income groups to low-income consumers will raise the level of aggregate demand and the level of income. This is also because the high-income groups have a lower MPC than low-income groups, given that MPC declines as income increases (for an empirical investigation of MPCs for different classes of income, see Venieris & Gupta, 1986). The case for progressive taxation as an instrument of income redistribution is also justified from this argument (Bunting, 1989; Krueger, 2012). In general and as Sheila Dow states:

'Keynesian policy' is popularly identified with his advocacy of particular short-run fiscal policy measures, his long-run focus was on establishing institutions to contribute to the state's necessary involvement in the economy, especially with respect to capital investment and income distribution. (Dow, 2023, p. 180)

Concluding Comments

Keynes' approach to consumption patterns plays a major role in his overall economic analysis. For Keynes, current income is the major determinant of consumption and the marginal propensity to consume determines the magnitudes of the multipliers. Keynes employed a largely psychological analysis of consumption, rejecting the model of utility maximising consumer. In Keynes' framework, changes in income will bring significant changes in consumption. These changes will be large and occur within a short time span, and this means that fiscal policy can be used as a major instrument in order to curb unemployment and economic recessions. Subsequently and until the first post-WWII decades, the Keynesian-based formulations of the consumption function became standard. The policy implications of Keynesian consumption analysis pointed towards a strong role of fiscal policy for macroeconomic stabilisation. They also supported the case for progressive taxation as an instrument of income redistribution. Almost immediately after Keynes' work on consumption, there were the first attempts to test it empirically, as will be discussed in the following chapter.

References

Akerlof, G., & Shiller, R. (2009). *Animal Spirits: How Human Psychology Drives the Economy, and Why It Matters for Global Capitalism.* Princeton University Press.

Arena, R., & Nasica, E. (2021). Keynes's Methodology and the Analysis of Economic Agent Behavior in a Complex World. *Revue d'économie Politique, 131*(3), 371–402.

Bruni, L., & Sugden, R. (2007). The Road Not Taken: How Psychology was Removed from Economics, and How It Might Be Brought Back. *The Economic Journal, 117*, 146–173.

Bunting, D. (1989). The Consumption Function 'Paradox'. *Journal of Post Keynesian Economics, 11*(3), 347–359.

Carabelli, A. (1988). *On Keynes's Method.* Macmillan.

Chick, V., & Jespersen, J. (2023). Holism and the Fallacy of Composition in Macroeconomics. In J. Jespersen, V. Chick, & B. Tieben (Eds.), *Routledge Handbook of Macroeconomic Methodology* (pp. 54–63). Routledge.

D'Orlando, F., & Sanfilippo, E. (2010). Behavioral Foundations for the Keynesian Consumption Function. *Journal of Economic Psychology, 31*(6), 1035–1046.

Davis, J. (2009). *Keynes's Philosophical Development.* Cambridge University Press.

Dimand, R. (1988). *The Origins of the Keynesian Revolution.* Edward Elgar.

Dow, S. (2012). Keynes on Knowledge, Expectations, and Rationality. In R. Frydman & E. Phelps (Eds.), *Rethinking Expectations: The Way Forward for Macroeconomics* (pp. 112–129). Princeton.

Dow, S. (2023). Keynes on Theorising for Policy. In S. A. Drakopoulos & I. Katselidis (Eds.), *Economic Policy and the History of Economic Thought* (pp. 173–187). Routledge.

Dow, S., & Dow, A. (2012). Animal Spirits and Rationality. In S. Dow (Ed.), *Foundations for New Economic Thinking: A Collection of Essays* (pp. 33–51). Palgrave Macmillan.

Dow, S., & Hillard, J. (Eds.). (1995). *Keynes, Knowledge and Uncertainty.* Edward Elgar.

Drakopoulos, S. (1992). Keynes's Economic Thought and the Theory of Consumer Behaviour. *Scottish Journal of Political Economy, 39*(3), 318–336.

Drakopoulos, S. (2021). The Marginalization of Absolute and Relative Income Hypotheses of Consumption and the Role of Fiscal Policy. *THE European Journal of the History of Economic Thought, 28*(6), 965–984.

Drakopoulos, S., & Katselidis, I. (2015). From Edgeworth to Econophysics: A Methodological Perspective. *Journal of Economic Methodology, 22*(1), 77–95.

Edgeworth, F. Y. (1881). *Mathematical Psychics: An Essay of the Application of Mathematics to Moral Sciences.* Kegan Paul.

Ferrari-Filho, F., & Conceição, O. (2005). The Concept of Uncertainty in Post Keynesian Theory and in Institutional Economics. *Journal of Economic Issues, 39*(3), 579–594.

Fisher, I. (1930). *The Theory of Interest.* Macmillan.

Galbacs, P. (2015). *The Theory of New Classical Macroeconomics: A Positive Critique.* Springer.

Goodwin, C. (2016). Economics and Psychology: Why the Great Divide? *History of Political Economy, 48*(suppl. 1), 71–169.

Keynes, J. M. (1921)[1972]. *The Collected Writings of John Maynard Keynes, Vol. VIII: A Treatise on Probability*: Macmillan.

Keynes, J. M. (1933)[1972]. *The Collected Writings of John Maynard Keynes, Vol. X: Essays in Biography.* Macmillan.

Keynes, J. M. (1936). *The General Theory of Employment, Interest, and Money.* Macmillan.

Keynes, J. M. (1937). The General Theory of Employment. *The Quarterly Journal of Economics, 51*(2), 209–223.

Komine, A. (2023). The Unfinished Revolution in Policy: The Visionary Legacy of Lord Keynes. In S. Drakopoulos & I. Katselidis (Eds.), *Economic Policy and the History of Economic Thought* (pp. 189–205). Routledge.

Krueger, A. (2012, January 12). The Rise and Consequences of Inequality in the United States. *Council of Economic Advisers Address.*

Lavoie, M. (1994). A Post Keynesian Theory of Consumer Choice. *Journal of Post Keynesian Economics, 16*(4), 539–562.

Lawson, T. (1988). Probability and Uncertainty in Economic Analysis. *Journal of Post Keynesian Economics, 11*(1), 38–65.

Lewin, S. (1996). Economics and Psychology: Lessons for Our Own Day from the Early Twentieth Century. *Journal of Economic Literature, 34*, 1293–1323.

Mason, R. (1995). Interpersonal Effects on Consumer Demand in Economic Theory and Marketing Thought, 1890–1950. *Journal of Economic Issues, 29*, 871–881.

Minsky, H. (1975). *John Maynard Keynes.* Columbia University Press.

O'Donnell, R. (1989). *Keynes: Philosophy, Economics and Politics.* Macmillan.

O'Donnell, R. (2018). Clarifying Keynes's Theory of Consumption and Psychological Law. *History of Economics Review, 71*(1), 94–117.

Pignalosa, D. (2021). The Euler Equation Approach: Critical Implications of Recent Developments in the Theory of Intertemporal Choice. *Bulletin of Political Economy, 15*(1), 1–43.

Radner, R. (1968). Competitive Equilibrium Under Uncertainty. *Econometrica, 36*, 31–58.

Roncaglia, A. (2009). Keynes and Probability: An Assessment. *European Journal of the History of Economic Thought, 16*(3), 489–510.

Savage, L. (1962). *The Foundations of Statistical Inference.* Methuen and Co.

Skidelsky, R. (1992). *John Maynard Keynes: The Economist as Saviour 1920–1937.* Macmillan.

Skidelsky, R. (1996). *Keynes.* Oxford University Press.

Snowdon, B., & Vane, H. (2005). *Modern Macroeconomics: Its Origins, Development and Current State.* Edward Elgar.

Venieris, Y., & Gupta, D. (1986). Income Distribution and Sociopolitical Instability as Determinants of Savings: A Cross-Sectional Model. *Journal of Political Economy, 94*(41), 873–883.

Wright, A. (1956). The Genesis of the Multiplier Theory. *Oxford Economic Papers, 8*(2), 181–193.

CHAPTER 4

Early Empirical Testing of Consumption Function and the Kuznets' Paradox

Introduction

Apart from the enormous impact of Keynes' theory, his work also inspired researchers in the emerging field of econometrics to focus on the newly invented national income and product statistics in order to test the empirical implications of Keynes' consumption analysis. The Keynesian approach to consumption implied the following empirical regularities: consumption expenditures can be expressed as a stable function of real income; the marginal propensity to consume (MPC) is positive but less than one; the marginal propensity to consume is lower than the average propensity to consume (APC); and that the marginal propensity to consume decreases as income increases. Consequently and soon after the spread of Keynes' ideas, there were the first empirical estimations of the absolute income hypothesis (AIH) based on cross-section data and time-series data (Ackley, 1961). Many researchers, including Lawrence Klein and Paul Samuelson, begun to test Keynes' absolute income hypothesis. One very influential study was by Simon Kuznets (1942, 1946) who analysed the characteristics of the consumption function based on his detailed reconstruction of US historical data on economic aggregates. Kuznets' studies initiated a whole literature focusing on the empirical testing of aggregate consumption patterns. The proliferation of the empirical works was accompanied by studies attempting to cast Keynes' theory into a more standard analytical framework. The IS-LM model suggested by John Hicks, which

S. A. Drakopoulos, *The Consumption Function in Economics*, https://doi.org/10.1007/978-3-032-15958-8_4

portrayed simultaneous equilibrium in the product and the money markets, was the main example (Hicks, 1937; see also Eichengreen, 2020). Modified by Franco Modigliani (1944) and popularised by Alvin Hansen (1953), the IS-LM model became the baseline tool of Keynesian macroeconomics (see also Snowdon & Vane, 2005).

This chapter will start with a discussion of the background of the first attempts to test the Keynesian consumption function. It will proceed with Simon Kuznets' "Consumption Paradox" referring to difference between the long-run and the short-run behaviour of the consumers' consumption patterns. It will finish with the early empirical dimensions of the paradox also focusing on subsequent interpretations of its econometric methodology.

Empirical Testing of Keynesian Consumption Function

Very soon after the publication of Keynes' theory, there were the first attempts to test his consumption function implications. The bulk of such work emerged in the US employing US data. Two types of data were used to test the Keynesian absolute income hypothesis: cross-section data (or budget), and time-series data. In particular, cross-section data was used to test the relation:

$$c_j = c_j\left(y_j, x_{1j}, x_{2j}, x_{3j}, \ldots x_{nj}\right) \quad (4.1)$$

In Eqn. (4.1), c_j is the consumption expenditures of the jth individual, y_j is the individual's level of income, and x_{nj} are the variables representing n characteristics of each of the individuals. Time-series data was used in testing an alternative specification of the consumption function:

$$C_t = C\left(Y_t, X_{1t}, X_{2t}, X_{3t}, \ldots X_{mt}\right) \quad (4.2)$$

In Eqn. (4.2), C_t is the sum of real consumption expenditures of some group of individuals at time t, Y_t is the combined income of that group, and X_{it} are characteristics of the group as a whole (Venieris & Sebold, 1977, pp. 363–365).

The first empirical estimations of Keynes' consumption function using aggregate time-series data indicated a value of the MPC around 0.75. More specifically, on the basis of annual US data for the period 1929–1941, the estimated consumption function was reported being $C_t = 26.6 + 0.75Y_t$ (Ackley, 1961, p. 225). Further, the availability of the US budget data on the consumption, savings, and income of individuals and families made it possible to test consumption patterns. These budget studies indicated a non-proportional relationship between family income and family consumption. In other words, they showed that APC falls as income increases. They also pointed to a positive value of autonomous consumption and confirmed the previous theoretical results that the MPC was less than the APC.

Lawrence Klein was one of the prominent early defenders of the theoretical and empirical aspects of the Keynesian consumption function (Klein, 1947a, 1947b). This was part of Klein's wider effort to test empirically the Keynesian macroeconomic system and paved the way for a new field of research: macroeconometric modelling (Visco, 2014). His subsequent econometric work with A. Klein and Coldberger (1955) supplied further empirical support to Keynes' approach. Regarding the Keynesian consumption function, Klein's strategy was to "envisage different possible factors that might influence consumption or saving, exploring whether they exert an effect and hence should be included in the model" (De Vroey & Malgrange, 2012, p. 126).

In the same vein, Paul Samuelson reviewing the early budget studies testing the Keynesian consumption function stated that "the consistency of the results is impressive, suggesting that here we have a fairly stable and fundamental relationship" (Samuelson, 1943, p. 28). Samuelson also studied the behaviour of the marginal propensity to consume during the business cycles, concluding that the MPC is higher during expansions than during recessions (Samuelson, 1943, pp. 33–34).[1] In fact, it has been argued that Samuelson's article can be seen as an initial attempt to consider the macroeconomic effects of the social significance of consumption expenditure (Trezzini, 2005, pp. 18–21; see also Pignalosa, 2025). Milton Friedman's assessment was also positive. As he wrote:

> *Both sources of data seemed at first to confirm Keynes' hypothesis. Current consumption expenditure was highly correlated with income, the marginal propensity to consume was less than unity, and the marginal propensity was less than the average propensity to consume, so the percentage of income saved increased with income.* (Friedman, 1957, pp. 3–4)

[1] Similar to Samuelson, Woytinsky (1946) argued that consumers' expenditures patterns during prosperity diverge markedly from the patterns in depression.

Thus the pattern observed in cross-sectional consumption data meant that at a given point in time, the rich in the population saved a higher fraction of their income than did the poor (see Koçkesen, 2008). In this framework, saving can be viewed as a 'luxury' good, whose share of overall income rises as people received higher incomes (Venieris & Sebold, 1977, p. 365).

An early article published in 1938 by Richard and Winifred Mary Stone was also designed to test the realism of Keynes' consumption function and the stability of the multiplier (Stone & Stone, 1938). Studying the relationship between consumption (*C*) and income (*Y*), they observed the likelihood of a 'standard of living effect', which would lessen a family's change in consumption in the event of an increase or decrease in its income; "the existence of a time trend in the relationship between *C* and *Y*; and the contradiction between the curvilinear relationship between *C* and *Y* suggested by budget studies and the linear relationship indicated by time-series" (Hagen, 1955, p. 48). This apparent contradiction was not emphasised initially, but it became central in subsequent empirical studies, and especially in Simon Kuznets' work.[2]

Simon Kuznets and the Consumption Paradox

Continuing the empirical work mentioned in the previous section, the American economist Simon Kuznets studied the characteristics of the consumption function based on his detailed reconstruction of US historical data on economic aggregates in the mid-1940s. Kuznets earned a PhD in 1926 at Columbia University under the supervision of the well-known Institutional economist Wesley Clair Mitchell. One of his main research interests was on economic fluctuations where he set the basis for a systematic analysis of business cycles. His work also provided empirical foundations to the Keynesian theory and played an important role in the dissemination of Keynesian policies after WWII. Kuznets tended to analyse the economy in connection with the wider context of historical, demographic, and social processes, an approach which is attributed to his early research experience in his native country.[3] In the framework of his studies on the formation of national income, Kuznets revealed long-term trends

[2] For a review of the debate regarding the econometric specification and the empirical results of the consumption function in the US during the 1940s, see Bronfenbrenner (1948).

[3] Russian born and educated, Kuznets became exposed to Joseph Schumpeter's theory of innovation and the business cycle (Pressman, 2006).

of output and income, consumption and savings, net investment, and so on (Lundberg, 1971; Drakopoulos, 2021).[4]

In 1942 there appeared Kuznets' series for net national product and net capital formation (equals savings) for overlapping decades from 1879–1888 to 1929–1938. In Kuznets' (1942) work, data both permitted and required analysis which took cognizance of changes over time. Their appearance marks the beginning of the second stage in empirical work concerning the consumption function (see also Hagen, 1955). Kuznets' (1946) subsequent work estimated aggregate consumption and income for the period of 1869 to 1938. His results indicated that the share of income consumed seemed to remain constant. Using overlapping decade averages of consumption and GDP, Kuznets showed that except for the years of the Great Depression (1929–1933), the APC in the US over the period 1869–1938 fluctuated narrowly between 0.84 and 0.89 (Kuznets, 1946). In other words, consumption and income tend to be proportionally related over a very long span of time-series data. Although the two sets of empirical evidence are not necessarily inconsistent, Kuznets' findings suggested that the long-run behaviour of the consumers might differ from their short-run consumption patterns. This inconsistency became known as Kuznets Paradox. Specifically, if MPC < APC as the OLS estimates of the linear consumption function suggested, then the share of income consumed should have declined as income increased, something that it was not shown by the long-run data. Thus, short-run econometric studies found MPC < APC while long-run data showed that MPC = APC. The following Fig. 4.1 explains Kuznets' approach.

In Fig. 4.1, the vertical axis (C) shows consumption expenditures and the horizontal axis (Y) shows real disposable income. The two short-run consumption functions flatter lines are labelled C_{SR1} and C_{SR2}. Line C_{SR1} might represent the cross-section consumption function of a low-income group and line C_{SR2} might represent the high-income group. As incomes of both groups rise over time, both lines would tend to slide up the steeper long-run consumption function, with the average household in each group tending to spend a constant share of its income over time. The long-run consumption function (C_{LR}) has a slope equal to the long-run APC (and MPC). The short-run consumption functions (C_{SR1}, C_{SR2}) have a slope (MPC) that is smaller than the APC. Kuznets' empirical results suggested a consumption function of the form:

[4] One of his most influential insights for subsequent research was the Kuznets curve, an inverted U-shaped relation between income inequality and economic growth (Kuznets, 1955).

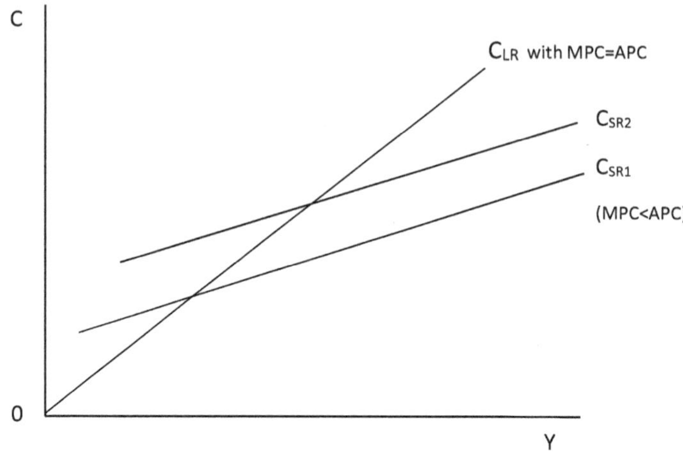

Fig. 4.1 Short-run and long-run consumption functions

$$C = kY \, with \, 0 < k < 1 \tag{4.3}$$

In Eqn. (4.3), Y is income, C is consumption, and k is a positive but less than 1 constant. The consumption function implies that MPC = APC = k. Further, the value of the MPC is much higher in Kuznets' function compared to Keynes' (Koçkesen, 2008; Palley, 2010).

Finally, there was another alleged inconsistency regarding the income elasticity of consumption (N_{cy}), which is defined in Eqn. (4.4) as:

$$N_{cy} = \left[\frac{dC}{dY}\right]\left[\frac{Y}{C}\right] \tag{4.4}$$

In Eqn. (4.4), N_{cy} is the income elasticity of consumption, Y is income, and C is consumption. Using US data, the average propensity to consume has remained at around 0.9 since 1900. This implied a long-run elasticity of income of about 1 and a constant saving rate. However, the cross-sectional data showed an elasticity of much less than one implying an increasing savings rate (for a discussion, see Bunting, 1989). Importantly, Friedman thought that these empirical findings undermined the notion of a stable relation between consumption and income and therefore Keynes' approach to consumption (Friedman, 1957).

The apparently conflicting empirical evidence was the main reason for subsequent attempts towards a consumption theory that would provide a reconciliation between the two sets of findings (see Hagen, 1955; Hynes, 1998). A notable attempt was by Arthur Smithies (1945) who tested Keynes' absolute income hypothesis in separate studies and concluded that the short-run relationship between consumption and income is non-proportional, but the time-series data showed the long-run relationship to be proportional. Smithies attempted to explain this inconsistency by introducing a time trend term pointing to the existence of an upward shift or "drift" in the short-run non-proportional consumption function due to factors other than income. These factors were (a) Migration from farms to cities probably increases the spending of the migrants; (b) A trend in the direction of a more equal distribution of income; and (c) Rising living standards have increased minimum costs of living. The rational was that the average saving-income ratio does tend to rise as income rises, but that other forces tend to reduce saving over time (Smithies, 1945; see also Hagen, 1955). Another early theoretical approach was the relative income hypothesis by James Duesenberry, which will be presented in the next chapter.[5] Further, Kuznets' findings led to new theories of consumption patterns suggested mainly by Milton Friedman and Franco Modigliani, which were based on mainstream microeconomic theory, and specifically on utility maximising and forward-looking agents. As will be seen in Chap. 6, these theories were very critical of Keynes' psychological approach to consumption.

The Early Empirical Dimensions of the Kuznets' Paradox

Subsequent specialised literature has cast serious doubts on the early empirical findings regarding the Keynesian consumption function. More specifically and by the late 1940s and early 1950s, issues relating to consumption patterns were considered to be 'stylized facts' to be explained by further research. In summary these were:

[5] James Tobin had also tested the relative income hypothesis against the absolute income hypothesis. His explanation will be discussed in a subsequent chapter (Tobin, 1951).

(a) the Absolute Income Hypothesis (AIH) empirical consumption functions were unstable,
(b) the APC was constant over long periods,
(c) short-run consumption functions tended to confirm the AIH but long-run estimates seemed to reject it,
(d) cross-section estimates of the MPC were systematically lower than time-series estimates, and appeared to shift upwards over time (Spanos, 1989, p. 157).

In the early 1950s, a number of works that focused on the empirical testing (and predicting) aggregate consumption patterns were published. For instance, Tom Davis (1952) categorised the consumption function formulations into three groups and attempted to test empirically their predicted and observed values, with rather disappointing results. Leo Fishman (1954) was critical of the empirical specifications of testing the consumption functions, emphasising the neglect of the role of consumer expectations. Almost three decades later, a number of subsequent works have focused on the statistical and econometric specifications of the early empirical papers testing the AIH. For instance, Aris Spanos' assessment was the following:

> *On closer examination the apparent paradoxes of the "stylized history" turn out to be either erroneous interpretations of the evidence or they are easily explainable on statistical grounds. In a nutshell the argument is that the textbook methodology led to a search for theory solutions to problems largely statistical in nature.* (Spanos, 1989, p. 151)

Spanos argued that in the light of recent developments in the methodology and practice of econometric modelling, the 'stylized facts' associated with the early literature were based on seriously mis-specified statistical models (Spanos, 1989, p. 168).

In the same vein, David Bunting (1989, 2003) argued that the discrepancies found by the early econometric works were more the result of statistical considerations than fundamental differences in economic behaviour (see also Mayer, 1972). For example, all cross-sectional studies involve household or family spending behaviour while the long-run studies deal with aggregate behaviour (Bunting, 1989, p. 349). Bunting concluded that his empirical results indicate that Keynes' 'fundamental law' is valid (Bunting, 1989, p. 358). Similar conclusions are reached in his subsequent work:

> *individual and average spending behavior were confused, causing incorrect implications to be derived from the consumption function implied by Keynes' Law. The effects of different types of consumer units on estimates of consumption were ignored, again causing confusion about spending behavior.* (Bunting, 2001, p. 151)

J. J. Thomas (1989) also focused on the econometric methodology of early studies on consumption. His central thesis was that the standard history of the early studies which casted doubt on Keynes' insights is misleading. In his words:

> *Many of the early studies of the consumption function reported in Table Al are unsophisticated by modern econometric standards, since the majority involve single equation estimation by ordinary least squares and usually only parameter estimates are reported without standard errors or other supporting statistical information.* (Thomas, 1989, p. 142)

A more general assessment of the early history of the empirical testing of consumption patterns has been offered by Thomas Mayer, who doubted that empirical testing had provided any clear-cut answers to the issue. As he wrote:

> *The 'plethora' of conflicting empirical evidence is such that an economist can decide on the basis of personal likes and dislikes whether he wants to accept or reject these new theories of the consumption function, and he can then find numerous empirical tests which will support and justify his chosen point of view.* (Mayer, 1972, p. 4)

In the same vein and almost 25 years later, Allan Hynes emphasised the problematic epistemological dimensions of testing aggregate consumption: "...if economics is a serious empirical science, an explanation of aggregate consumption would seem to be a straight-forward task, almost mundane, but the record suggests otherwise" (Hynes, 1998, pp. 27–28).

Concluding Comments

Keynes' approach to consumption and its implications initiated a plethora of empirical studies using time-series and cross-sectional US data. Most of these studies focused on testing the absolute income hypothesis and its theoretical consequences. One of the most influential studies was by

Simon Kuznets who found an apparent inconsistency between the long-run consumption function and the short-run consumption function (Kuznets Paradox). Although subsequent studies have spotted some serious problems regarding the econometric methodology of many works testing the Kuznets Paradox, the controversy concerning Keynes' consumption set the basis for the emergence of alternative consumption functions. The one suggested by James Duesenberry is the subject of the next chapter. The controversy also provided the impetus for the construction of consumption functions based on standard microeconomic foundations (i.e. the utility maximising model), which eventually undermined and displaced the Keynesian approach to consumption.

References

Ackley, G. (1961). *Macroeconomic Theory.* Macmillan.

Bronfenbrenner, M. (1948). The Consumption Function Controversy. *Southern Economic Journal, 14*(3), 304–320.

Bunting, D. (1989). The Consumption Function 'Paradox'. *Journal of Post Keynesian Economics, 11*(3), 347–359.

Bunting, D. (2001). Keynes's Law and Its Critics. *Journal of Post Keynesian Economics, 24*, 149–163.

Bunting, D. (2003). Consumption. In J. King (Ed.), *The Elgar Companion to Post Keynesian Economics* (pp. 72–76). Edward Elgar.

Davis, T. (1952). The Consumption Function as a Tool for Prediction. *The Review of Economics and Statistics, 34*(3), 270–277.

De Vroey, M., & Malgrange, P. (2012). From the 'Keynesian Revolution' to the Klein-Goldberger Model: Klein and the Dynamization of Keynesian Theory. *History of Economic Ideas, 20*(2), 113–135.

Drakopoulos, S. (2021). Theories of Consumption. In L.-P. Rochon & S. Rosi (Eds.), *An Introduction to Macroeconomics* (pp. 233–267). Edward Elgar.

Eichengreen, B. (2020). Keynesian Economics: Can it Return if it Never Died? *Review of Keynesian Economics, 8*(1), 23–35.

Fishman, L. (1954). Consumer Expectations and the Consumption Function. *Southern Economic Journal, 20*(3), 243–251.

Friedman, M. (1957). *The Consumption Function.* Princeton University Press.

Hagen, E. (1955). The Consumption Function: A Review Article. *The Review of Economic and Statistics, 37*(1), 48–54.

Hansen, A. (1953). *A Guide to Keynes.* McGraw-Hill.

Hicks, J. (1937). Mr. Keynes and the 'Classics'. *Econometrica, 5*, 147–159.

Hynes, A. H. (1998). The Emergence of the Neoclassical Consumption Function: The Formative Years. 1940–1952. *Journal of the History of Economic Thought, 20*(01), 25–49.

Klein, L. (1947a). The Use of Econometric Models as a Guide to Economic Policy. *Econometrica, 15*(2), 111–151.

Klein, L. (1947b). *The Keynesian Revolution*. Macmillan.

Klein, L., & Coldberger, A. (1955). *An Econometric Model of the United States, 1929–1942*. North-Holland.

Koçkesen, L. (2008). The Relative Income Hypothesis. In W. A. Darity (Ed.), *International Encyclopedia of the Social Sciences* (2nd ed., pp. 153–154). Macmillan.

Kuznets, S. (1942). *Uses of National Income in Peace and War*. National Bureau of Economic Research.

Kuznets, S. (1946). *National Product Since 1869* (assisted by L. Epstein and E. Zenks). National Bureau of Economic Research.

Kuznets, S. (1955). Economic Growth and Income Inequality. *American Economic Review, 45*, 1–28.

Lundberg, E. (1971). Simon Kuznets Contributions to Economics. *The Swedish Journal of Economics, 73*(4), 444–459.

Mayer, T. (1972). *Permanent Income, Wealth and Consumption: A Critique of the Permanent Income Theory, the Life-Cycle Hypothesis and Related Theories*. University of California Press.

Modigliani, F. (1944). Liquidity Preference and the Theory of Interest and Money. *Econometrica, 12*, 44–88.

Palley, T. (2010). Relative Permanent Income Theory of Consumption: A Synthetic Keynes- Duesenberry- Friedman Model. *Review of Political Economy, 22*(1), 41–56.

Pignalosa, D. (2025). Consumption as a Social Phenomenon in the Modern Theory of Intertemporal Choice. *Review of Political Economy, 37*(2), 543–563.

Pressman, S. (2006). *Fifty Major Economists*. Routledge.

Samuelson, P. (1943). Full Employment After the War. In S. E. Harris (Ed.), *Postwar Economic Problems* (pp. 27–53). McGraw Hill.

Smithies, A. (1945). Forecasting Postwar Demand. *Econometrica, 13*, 1–14.

Snowdon, B., & Vane, H. (2005). *Modern Macroeconomics: Its Origins, Development and Current State*. Edward Elgar.

Spanos, A. (1989). Early Empirical Findings on the Consumption Function, Stylized Facts or Fiction: A Retrospective View. *Oxford Economic Papers, 41*, 150–169.

Stone, R., & Stone, W. (1938). The Marginal Propensity to Consume and the Multi- plier. *Review of Economic Studies, 6*, 1–24.

Thomas, J. (1989). The Early Econometric History of the Consumption Function. *Oxford Economic Papers, 41*, 131–149.

Tobin, J. (1951). Relative Income, Absolute Income, and Saving. Reprinted in *Essays in Economics, 2: Consumption and Econometrics,* Cambridge: MIT Press, 1987.

Trezzini, A. (2005). The Economics of Consumption as a Social Phenomenon: A Neglected Approach to the Analysis of Consumption. *Quaderno di ricerca* n. 2, DIeS Dipartimento Innovazione e Societa` Roma*:* 1–36.

Venieris, Y., & Sebold, F. (1977). *Macroeconomics: Models and Policy.* John Wiley & Sons.

Visco, I. (2014). Lawrence R. Klein: Macroeconomics, Econometrics and Economic Policy. *Journal of Policy Modeling, 36*, 605–628.

Woytinsky, W. (1946). Relationship Between Consumers' Expenditures, Savings, and Disposable Income. *The Review of Economics and Statistics, 28*(1), 1–12.

CHAPTER 5

The Social Significance of Consumption: James Duesenberry and Harvey Leibenstein

Introduction

Chapter 3 argued that Keynes' approach to consumption patterns exhibited a strong psychological and sociological dimension. Following Kuznets' empirical findings, James Duesenberry (1949) introduced his *Relative Income Hypothesis* (RIH), a theoretical construction which was also characterised by a strong psychological and sociological dimension. Clearly influenced by Veblen's ideas, his approach to consumption is also sometimes described as a pioneer in establishing microeconomic foundations for the Keynesian consumption function (see, for instance, Hynes, 1998, p. 39; Hoover, 2010, pp. 28–32). During the same period and following Duesenberry's work, Harvey Leibenstein's (1950) theory of consumer behaviour was heavily based on notions from psychology and especially from social psychology. Similar to Duesenberry, Leibenstein rejected the core mainstream assumption that individual's preferences are independent. Although Leibenstein focused on microeconomics, his work provided further theoretical foundations to the conception of consumption as a social phenomenon.

This chapter will start with an outline of the social significance of consumption of Duesenberry's theory. It will proceed with his critique of the fundamental assumptions of mainstream demand theory and to a discussion of his Relative Income Hypothesis, including the *demonstration* and the *ratchet* effects. The demonstration effect applies when a household's

S. A. Drakopoulos, *The Consumption Function in Economics*,
https://doi.org/10.1007/978-3-032-15958-8_5

consumption depends not just on its own current level of income, but on its income relative to those in the subgroup of the population with which it identifies itself. Further, a household that has in the past achieved income levels higher than its present levels would attempt to maintain the high consumption levels that it achieved earlier (the ratchet effect). It will finish with a presentation of Leibenstein's ideas on social status and consumption. There will also be a brief discussion of George Katona's views who was placing emphasis on the psychological aspects of consumption decisions.

James Duesenberry: The Social Significance of Consumption

James Duesenberry in his *Income, Saving and the Theory of Consumer Behaviour* (1949) made one of the first attempts aimed at providing a theoretical justification for the discrepancy between Kuznets's short-run and the long-run empirical findings on consumption. Duesenberry suggested the relative income hypothesis as the main theory underlying the consumption function findings. The hypothesis introduces psychological and sociological factors such as social interdependencies and habit formation to the study of consumer behaviour (see also Hynes, 1998, pp. 41–42). The role of social comparisons was not a new idea. The view that people compare their income, consumption, or wealth with other people's income, consumption, or wealth can be found in many major economists such as Adam Smith, Karl Marx, John Stuart Mill, Thorstein Veblen, and Arthur Cecil Pigou (see Drakopoulos, 2016). Its specific application to consumption patterns was developed by Thorstein Veblen and Hazel Kyrk as was seen in Chap. 2. Duesenberry, however, was the first to apply the notion of social comparisons to the study of consumption in a systematic manner. In fact, Duesenberry's work can be viewed as a continuation of Veblen's ideas, given that there are many common points concerning income and consumption comparisons, and also concerning the role of the demonstration effect (see McCormick, 1983 and the subsequent section). Further, an important common point between Duesenberry's and Keynes's approaches to consumption was the concept of social comparisons or relative standing: Duesenberry put emphasis on relative consumption, while Keynes emphasised relative wage. Although Keynes recognised the importance of social influences on consumption decisions, he did not develop them further in his *General Theory*, arguing that they were stable, at least in the short-run (see Keynes, 1936; Mason, 2000). Duesenberry's consumption theory was explicitly based on the role of social comparisons in economic decisions, and thus the social significance of consumption was his central point (see also Barnett, 2024).[1]

Critique of Fundamental Assumptions of Demand Theory

In his 1949 book, Duesenberry started by claiming that two 'fundamental assumptions' of demand theory are 'invalid'. These assumptions are:

> *(1) that every individual's consumption behaviour is independent of that of every other individual.*
> *(2) that consumption relations are reversible in time.* (Duesenberry, 1949, p. 1)

Concerning the core assumption of independent preferences of orthodox economics, Duesenberry asserted that it has "no empirical basis" and then stated that "there are strong psychological and sociological reasons for supposing that preferences are in fact interdependent" (Duesenberry, 1949, p. 3).[2] The clear implication in the context of consumption theory was that consumers will be influenced by the behaviour of other consumers:

> *any particular consumer will be influenced by consumption of people with whom he has social contacts.* (Duesenberry, 1949, p. 48)

This idea—labelled as the *demonstration effect*—questioned the established view that absolute levels of income only determine patterns of consumer demand (Duesenberry, 1949, p. 27). Consequently, he maintained that a household's consumption would depend not just on its own current level of income, but on its income relative to those in the subgroup of the population with which it identifies itself. The household will attempt to

[1] It has been argued that Dorothy Brady and Rose Friedman's paper (Brady & Friedman, 1947) was very important in the development of the relative income hypothesis, and, in a general scientific context, it was the first attempt to provide a unifying hypothesis of consumption data (Hynes, 1998, p. 29).

[2] For an analysis of interdependent preferences and their theoretical consequences, see Pollak (1976).

match its consumption behaviour, and thus its consumption expenditures with those of other members of its group. It follows that households with lower income within the group will consume a larger share of their income to 'keep up with the Joneses', while households with high incomes relative to the group will save more and consume less. Demonstrating a clear influence from Veblen, he argued:

> *We can maintain then that the frequency and strength of impulses to increase expenditure depends on frequency of contact with goods superior to those habitually consumed. This effect need not depend at all on considerations of emulation or "conspicuous consumption".* (Duesenberry, 1949, pp. 27–28)

Thus, the frequency and strength of impulses to increase expenditure depend on frequency of contact with goods superior to those habitually consumed. Duesenberry appealed to self-observation in order to support the presence of the demonstration effect. As he wrote:

> *The best way to demonstrate that consumption expenditures can be forced up by contact with superior consumption goods is to ask the reader to consult his own experience. What kind of reaction is produced by looking at a friend's new car or looking at houses or apartments better than one's own? The response is likely to be a feeling of dissatisfaction with one's own house or car. If this feeling is produced often enough it will lead to action, which eliminates it, that is, to increase expenditure.* (Duesenberry, 1949, p. 27)

The second basic component of Duesenberry's approach is the rejection of the standard notion that consumption relations are reversible in time (Duesenberry, 1949, p. 1). In his own words:

> *Over time, the relation between aggregate consumption and aggregate income is not completely reversible. As income increases secularly, consumption will grow proportionally; but over the cycle, as income falls from its peak, consumers will attempt to maintain consumption standards set previously.* (Duesenberry, 1949, p. 7)

The main difference from the demonstration effect is that instead of comparing their income to those of other households, each household is assumed to consider its current income relative to its own past income levels. A household that has in the past achieved income levels higher than its present levels would attempt to maintain the high consumption levels that it achieved earlier. Because of the strong influence of habits, consumption is slow to fall when income is reduced. More precisely:

> *The fundamental psychological postulate underlying our argument is that it is harder for a family to reduce its expenditure from a higher level than for a family to refrain from making high expenditures in the first place. Or, to put it differently, it is far easier to adjust to an upward that to a downward mobility.* (Duesenberry, 1948, p. 70)

Thus, consumption patterns are asymmetric in the sense that when incomes fall, consumption would not fall in proportion. The result of this behaviour for aggregate consumption is called the *ratchet effect.*

In spite of his clear influences from Institutionalism and especially from Veblen's approach, Duesenberry was not willing to abandon completely the marginalist tools as his discussion of the long-term average propensity to save (APS) indicates. Specifically, in his explanation of the constancy of the long-run propensity to save, Duesenberry used marginalist principles combined with Institutionalist assumptions (for a detailed analysis, see Trezzini, 2012; see also Duesenberry, 1949, pp. 14–15).[3]

The Relative Income Hypothesis

As was mentioned previously, Duesenberry attempted to find a solution to the Kuznets's paradox. In this context and given his rejection of the two fundamental assumptions of demand theory, Duesenberry proceeded to build his *Relative Income Hypothesis* (RIH). When consumers come frequently in contact with superior goods, they are constantly reminded of their low social status. The result will be "an increase in expenditure at the expense of saving" (Duesenberry, 1949, p. 27). Thus, households with lower income within the group will consume a larger share of their income to 'keep up with the Joneses', while households with high incomes relative

[3] Holländer (2001) has attempted to incorporate Duesenberry's idea in a standard utility framework as follows: The basic utility function can be written as $u(l, x)$, where l and x denote the individuals leisure and bundle of consumed commodities, respectively. The Duesenberry utility function can be written as $u(l, x, a)$, where a denotes the commodity bundle to which the individual aspires. It is, therefore, called the individuals aspirations or, synonymously, wants, desires, or needs. Utility is decreasing in aspirations, and a proportionate increase in desires and the means of their satisfaction leaves utility unchanged, that is, the utility function is homogeneous of degree zero in (x, a) (see Holländer, 2001).

to the group will save more and consume less. The demonstration effect can be understood better with reference to Fig. 5.1.

In Fig. 5.1, the vertical axis (C_m) shows family consumption expenditures and the horizontal axis (Υ_m) shows family real disposable income. Consumption schedules I, II, and III indicate the relationship between family income and family consumption at times 1, 2, and 3, respectively. For instance, consumption schedule I depicts this relationship at time t = 1 as $C_i = a_1 + b_1 \Upsilon_i$. The same reasoning holds for schedules II and III. The shape of this family consumption shows that within a distribution of income, the APC falls as we move from low-income to high-income families. This feature is consistent with both the Keynesian absolute income hypothesis and Duesenberry's relative income hypothesis. If we assume that all families receive proportional increases in income in period t = 2, the distribution of income remains the same. In terms of the absolute income hypothesis, this would mean a movement along consumption schedule I. In terms of relative income, this would mean that the consumption schedule will shift from I to II.

In particular, let us assume that in t = 1, mean family income is Υ_{m1}, and the corresponding level of consumption is C_{m1}. After the proportional increase in all incomes, the family will maintain its position in the income distribution by earning Υ_{m2} in t = 2, thus its APC will remain unchanged,

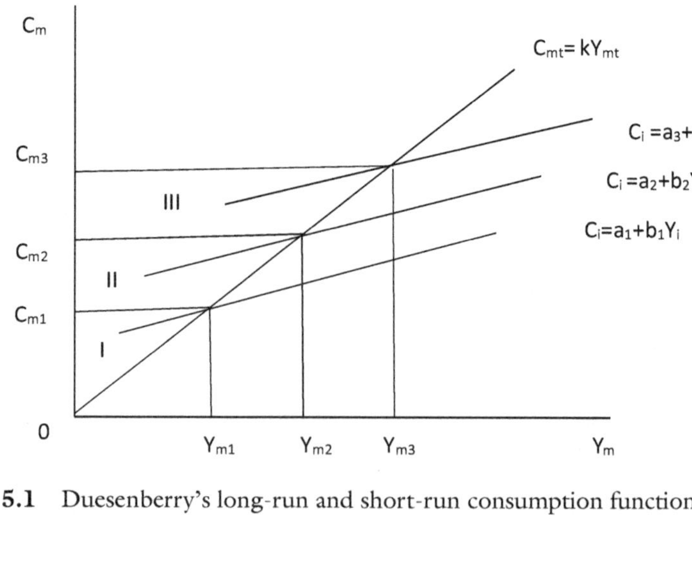

Fig. 5.1 Duesenberry's long-run and short-run consumption functions

resulting in a level of consumption at C_{m2}. The extension of this principle to all families gives consumption schedule II. If the same process is repeated in $t = 3$, we would derive consumption schedule III. In sum, a general proportional rise in the levels of income would cause successive cross-section studies to reveal shifts in family consumption schedule. As the consumption schedule shifts over long periods of time and with unchanged income distribution, the long-run time series will indicate a proportional relationship between aggregate consumption and aggregate income, given as $C_{mt} = kY_{mt}$. Thus, Duesenberry's approach was able to reconcile the apparently contradictory results of the budget studies and Kuznets' findings.

According to the relative income hypothesis, levels of expenditure could be increased not by changes in income or prices, but by following the consumption expenditures of others with whom the individual had contacts (Duesenberry, 1949, p. 29). In formal terms, Duesenberry's consumption function is:

$$Ct = kYt, \text{with } APC = \frac{Ct}{Yt} = k \tag{5.1}$$

In Eqn. (5.1), C_t is the real per capita consumption of year t, Y_t is the real per capita disposable income of year t, and k is a constant. In other words, the APC is constant in the long run, in accordance with Kuznets' findings (see also Venieris & Sebold, 1977, pp. 366–371).

In Duesenberry's work, aggregate consumption depends not only on current disposable income but also on the ratio of current income to previous peak level income. As he asserts: "saving depends on past as well as current income" (1949, p. 76). In other words, consumers may be slow to change their standard of living as quickly as income rises over the expansionary stage of the business cycle. Following Duesenberry's (1949, p. 7) formalisation, the consumption function in terms of the average propensity to consume (C_t/Y_t) is written as:

$$\frac{Ct}{Yt} = a - b\left(\frac{Yt}{Yo}\right) \tag{5.2}$$

In Eqn. (5.2), Y_t is the real per capita disposable income of year t, Y_0 is the previous peak of real per capita disposable income, and a, $b > 0$. The above implies a consumption function of the form:

$$Ct = aYt - b\left(\frac{Yt^2}{Yo}\right) \tag{5.3}$$

The theoretical implication of Eqn. (5.3) is that secular growth in income results in a constant long-run average propensity to consume: If income grows over the long run at an average rate of g per cent per year, the long-run ratio of current income to previous peak income would be:

$$\frac{Yt}{Yo} = (1+g) \tag{5.4}$$

Given Eqn. (5.4), the APC will be:

$$\frac{Ct}{Yo} = \alpha - b(1+g) = k \tag{5.5}$$

In Eqn. (5.5), k is a positive constant. Further, the MPC is given by Eqn. (5.6):

$$MPC = \frac{\partial C}{\partial Y} = a - 2b\left(\frac{Yt}{Yo}\right) = \alpha - 2b(1+g) \tag{5.6}$$

A comparison of Eqns. (5.5) and (5.6) shows that MPC < APC, a result which is in agreement with Keynes' views.

By referring to Fig. 5.1, when incomes rise, consumption increases along the steeper long-run consumption function. However, when a recession hits and incomes decline, households reduce consumption less than proportionally and fall back along the flatter short-run consumption function. During the recovery, they move up along the flat line until they reach their highest attained level of consumption. After recovery, when incomes grow again, they proceed up the long-run line again until the next recession, when they fall back along a flatter line. Thus, consumption ratchets upward, staying relatively near its highest past value when income declines. The implication is that in the long run, APC will be constant, but as the economy moves through the business cycle, the ratio of current to previous peak income will vary and thus APC will also follow the cyclical fluctuations. Duesenberry's theoretical approach was able to reconcile the discrepancy between the empirical cross-section studies and the long-run findings.

Duesenberry's main theoretical implication, that the APC will be greater than the MPC, lies solidly in the Keynesian tradition (Kosobud, 1998, p. 135). Further, Duesenberry's theory suggests that fiscal changes may have an asymmetrical effect. Tax reductions may well stimulate consumption spending. However, tax increases may not have a significant effect in curbing demand in the short-run, as consumers strive to maintain consumption levels (for a detailed discussion of tax policies when consumption is interdepended, see Duesenberry, 1949, pp. 96–102; Kosicki, 1990; Alvarez-Cuadrado & Long, 2011). In the same conceptual framework, it has been argued that relative consumption concerns may substantially increase the optimal marginal tax rate and that may induce substantially more redistribution. This entails that "an additional incentive for income redistribution from wealthy to poor citizens is created" (Boskin & Sheshinski, 1978, p. 590; see also McCormick, 2018). Under interdependency, progressive taxation for explicit redistributive purposes may be fully consistent with the Pareto criterion (Postlewaite, 1998; Corneo, 2002; for a review see also Truyts, 2010).[4] Finally, Duesenberry's views have important consequences for other theoretical issues like the pattern of savings and growth as Duesenberry himself intended. In this framework, savings rates depend on the position of income distribution and not exclusively on the income level, as in a traditional savings function.

Almost immediately after its publication, Duesenberry's work was acknowledged as a very important contribution to consumption theory by many leading economists of the period. Kenneth Arrow's book review in the *American Economic Review* was very positive, describing it as "one of the most significant contributions of the post-war period to our understanding of economic behaviour ... [and] in the best tradition of economic thought" (Arrow, 1950, p. 906).[5] Analogous positive views were expressed by G.L.S. Schackle and A.C. Pigou (see Mason, 2000).

Similarly, the position of leading consumption theory specialists such as Franco Modigliani towards interdependent consumption decisions and particularly towards their specific expression in Duesenberry's analysis was

[4] The literature on positional goods is an example of interdependent preferences. See, for instance, Frank (2008).

[5] It is interesting that Arrow mentions that Pigou and Rose Friedman had similar views to Duesenberry's concerning savings behavior (Arrow, 1950, pp. 908, 911).

initially sympathetic. Apart from Duesenberry's hypothesis, Modigliani was also supportive of T. Brown's formulation that "there is a definite lag or inertia to consumers' responses to current income changes", and in order to explain this inertia, "one has followed the theories of Modigliani and Duesenberry, in terms of consumers' memories of past heights or peaks of real income" (Brown, 1952, p. 370). In fact, Modigliani refers to a 'Duesenberry-Modigliani-Brown' hypothesis in his subsequent work (Modigliani, 1975, p. 4). Moreover, in a paper published in 1949, Modigliani embraced the idea of relative income effects on consumption in his own research by adopting a function in which aggregate consumption depends on current income, and on the difference between current income and the highest level of income attained in the past (Modigliani, 1949). His assumptions are formalised in the following consumption function:

$$Ct = aYt - \beta\left(Yt - Y_{\tau}^{o}\right) \tag{5.7}$$

In Eqn. (5.7), *Yt*, is real income of the year *t*, *Ct* is aggregate consumption at time t, Y_{τ}^{o} is the highest level of real income realised in any year preceding *t*, and α, $\beta > 0$. It is clear that since consumption depends on past income, the concept of relative income is the underling basis of the consumption function. The similarity between Duesenberry's and Modigliani's consumption functions (Eqns. (5.3) and (5.7)) is clear (see also Trezzini, 2005).

Harvey Leibenstein: Social Status and Consumption

James Duesenberry's work was not the only one in the first Post-WWII decades to focus on consumption as a social phenomenon. Harvey Leibenstein's theory of consumer behaviour was heavily based on notions from psychology and especially from social psychology. He is also considered to be one of the first economists to explore issues pertaining to what is called today behavioural economics (Frantz, 2004, 2020). Although he is basically known for his work in the theory of the firm (x-efficiency theory), Leibenstein's theory of consumer behaviour has been less popular but also important. Leibenstein's approach was not so much focused on macroeconomic theory and its policy implications, but more on microeconomic phenomena. Similar to Duesenberry, he challenged one of the established mainstream assumptions about individual economic behaviour, suggesting that an individual's preferences are not independent, but they are affected by the preferences of other individuals.[6] In his economic analysis, he frequently referred to the significant role of social psychology and to the psychological dimensions of economic behaviour (e.g. Leibenstein, 1950, pp. 184, 198–199, 202; Leibenstein, 1975, p. 9). In addition, he recognised that both previous and contemporary economists like Rae, Pigou, Cunynghame, Duesenberry, and Meade had considered the important issue of interdependence (Leibenstein, 1950). Moreover, it should be noted that the notions of social status and relative income are central in his microeconomic approach (Leibenstein, 1976). More generally, Leibenstein attempted to give microeconomics new psychological underpinnings by replacing economic man with "S.R." man—S.R. for selective rationality (Leibenstein, 1976, p. 268; see also Backhouse & Fontaine, 2018, p. 33).

In his early paper titled *Bandwagon, Snob, and Veblen Effects in the Theory of Consumers' Demand* (1950), Leibenstein aimed to relax "one of the basic implicit assumptions of the current theory—namely, that the consumption behaviour of any individual is independent of the consumption of others" (Leibenstein, 1950, p. 184). He proceeded to distinguish three possible cases of interdependency: the *bandwagon effect*, the *snob effect*, and the *Veblen effect*. The bandwagon effect refers to the extent to which the demand for a commodity is increased due to the fact that others are also consuming the same commodity. Its conceptual basis is the "desire of people to purchase a commodity in order to get into 'the swim of things'; in order to conform with the people they wish to be associated with; in order to be fashionable or stylish; or, in order to appear to be 'one of the boys'" (Leibenstein, 1950, p. 189). The main theoretical implication of the bandwagon effect is that the demand curve will be more elastic than if demand is based only on the functional attributes of the commodity. According to Leibenstein, the snob effect is the opposite of the bandwagon effect since it refers:

[6] A good part of Tibor Scitovsky's work was also focused on criticising the established approach to economic rationality arguing that interdependence among consumers is undoubtedly important (Scitovsky, 1954, p. 144). Similarly, J. K. Galbraith also attacked the orthodox view of consumer behaviour (Galbraith, 1958).

> *to the extent to which the demand for a consumers' good is decreased owing to the fact that others are also consuming the same commodity (or that others are increasing their consumption of that commodity). This represents the desire of people to be exclusive; to be different; to dissociate themselves from the "common herd".* (Leibenstein, 1950, p. 189)

Due to the snob effect, the demand curve will be less elastic than the demand curve where there are no snob effects. Finally, the Veblen effect refers "to the phenomenon of conspicuous consumption; to the extent to which the demand for a consumers' good is increased because it bears a higher rather than a lower price" (Leibenstein, 1950, p. 189). The presence of Veblen effect might produce demand curves which include negative and positive slopes. Realising the vital link of his analysis to psychological research, he stated:

> *The factors that would determine one set of expectations rather than the other are matters of empirical investigation in the field of social psychology.* (Leibenstein, 1950, p. 199)

Apart from the notion of interdependency in demand, Leibenstein applied his ideas regarding social status and preference interdependence in a study titled *The Economic Theory of Fertility Decline* published in 1975. In order to examine the factors affecting fertility decline, he employed the notions of social status, status goods, and consumption demonstration effects (see also Albanese, 2009).[7] In particular, he argued that fertility decline is caused by the achievement of higher social position which implies a higher proportion of household income to expenditures on status goods to reflect the new higher social class. He justified his points by referring to psychology. As he wrote:

> *We live in social groups. Beyond basic sustenance, consumption has a broad social status (lifestyle) basis.* (Leibenstein, 1975, p. 5)

The concept of social status refers to a household's relative position in the hierarchy of social status groups or the class structure of society. The concept of relative income refers to the income of a household relative to

[7] Similar to Duesenberry, the central role of social status is also visible in the economic analysis of Fred Hirsch (1931–1978), who provided the basis for the modern discussion of positional goods (Hirsch, 1976; see also Schneider, 2007).

the average income within a given social status group. Leibenstein elaborates on the concept of the relevant status group by employing the term *social influence group* or *SIG*. As he states:

> *Once the family agrees to live in a style somewhat similar to those who are in its SIG, many areas of discretion are narrowed. Family members with similar demographic characteristics (age, sex, etc.) will to some extent have to be equipped with similar material goods. The very meaning of belonging (and especially demonstrating belonging) to a given SIG implies some similarity in the type of expenditure patterns.* (Leibenstein, 1975, pp. 13–14)

Once a higher social status has been achieved, individuals would strive to preserve it. In his words: "Families try to maintain a strong status differential through their expenditure patterns" (Leibenstein, 1975, p. 6). The fear of moving to a lower status motivates families to limit family size (Leibenstein, 1975). The similarity with Duesenberry's arguments is clearly visible. In fact, Leibenstein acknowledged his influences from Duesenberry's relative consumption theory (see also Albanese, 2009). As he himself stated:

> *James Duesenberry, in his Income, Saving, And The Theory of Consumer Behavior, (...) discusses the relation between consumption and social status (see pp. 28–32). He argues as I do, that status expenditures are higher for higher income groups (p. 113).* (Leibenstein, 1975, p. 7, n. 11)

As mentioned above, Leibenstein's main concern was to utilise psychological concepts in his effort to provide new foundations to microeconomic theory (Leibenstein, 1976; see also Albanese, 1988). However, Leibenstein's contributions regarding social status considerations in consumption behaviour did not only support Duesenberry's argumentation, but also the entire line of reasoning on consumption found in Veblen, Kyrk, and Keynes.

During the same period, George Katona's psychological economics was in the same conceptual framework. Katona worked at the University of Michigan Survey Research Center on the impact of shifting consumer sentiment on discretionary consumer spending. The Center's Index of Consumer Sentiment attempted to forecast of automobile demand in the US. The construction of the index was based on a psychological model of human behaviour taking into consideration people's motives, attitudes, expectations, and aspirations (Katona, 1971). The inclusion of the above factors constituted the core of what he called *behavioral economics*: "Behavioral economics is a young discipline that must advance substantially in order to fulfill its promise to broaden the range of economic inquiry. By considering the human element in economic affairs, I believe, it will be possible to shed light on a variety of social problems and also to improve our forecasting tools" (Katona, 1971, p. 239).

More generally, Katona was strongly against any attempt to exclude psychological considerations from economics. In fact, he thought that psychology could supply "conceptual as well as methodological tools for the investigation of economic behavior" (Katona, 1951, pp. 3–4). In the same setting, he criticised the Keynesian analysis of consumption for not relying enough on psychological research. He suggested that instead of analysing consumption in relation to aggregate income, the analysis of consumer behaviour should rely on the more established psychological method of 'sample interview' (Katona, 1964, p. 45; see also Edwards, 2014, p. 701). Further, he was critical of Keynes' neglect of consumer income expectations as "a superficial conclusion drawn from experience in an earlier, very different, time" (Katona, 1946, p. 320).[8] He also dismissed Milton Friedman's permanent-income hypothesis of consumption as outmoded and not applicable to present-day economic conditions (King, 2016, pp. 69–71). Finally, it should be noted that although Katona's thinking about consumption had many common ideas to other non-orthodox economists of the period, he also had objections to the points put forward by 'social critics' of consumer affluence like Galbraith's, 1958 work (Edwards, 2014, p. 709; see also Chap. 10).

Concluding Comments

Clearly, Duesenberry's relative consumption theory can be placed in the long conceptual tradition of viewing consumption patterns and decisions as socially dependent phenomena. Together with Keynes' absolute income hypothesis, Duesenberry's theory offered additional justification for socially based consumption patterns. The works of Leibenstein and Katona also added support to the psychological and sociological dimensions of

[8] In spite of Katona's criticism of Keynes, John King (2016) argues that as far as theory of consumption expenditure is concerned, Katona and Keynes should be regarded as complements, not substitutes.

consumption. Furthermore, this tradition was at odds to the orthodox treatment of consumption in terms of economic rationality outcomes based on the core notion of preference independence.

The orthodox response to the social significance of consumption approaches was to employ the standard optimising framework that can be found in Fisher's intertemporal consumption choice. Milton Friedman's permanent-income hypothesis, and Franco Modigliani and Richard Brumberg's life-cycle hypothesis of consumption moved away from the social aspects of consumption, making standard individual rationality the foundation of consumption theories. As will be discussed in the next chapter, the economics orthodoxy to consumption became dominant. This paradigm shift had also considerable impact on economic policy prescriptions.

References

Albanese, P. (1988). The Formation and Change of Fertility Preferences. *Journal of Behavioral Economics, 17*, 35–55.

Albanese, P. (2009). Leibenstein's Theory of Consumption Behaviour. In R. Frantz (Ed.), *Renaissance in Behavioral Economics: Essays in Honour of Harvey Leibenstein* (pp. 194–210). Routledge.

Alvarez-Cuadrado, F., & Long, N. V. (2011). The Relative Income Hypothesis. *Journal of Economic Dynamics & Control, 35*, 1489–1501.

Arrow, K. (1950). Book Review of *Income, Saving and the Theory of Consumer Behaviour* (J. Duesenberry). *American Economic Review, 40*, 906–911.

Backhouse, R., & Fontaine, P. (2018). Economics and Other Social Sciences: A Historical Perspective. *Annals of the Fondazione Luigi Einaudi, LII*, 7–44.

Barnett, V. (2024). James Duesenberry (1918–2009). In R. A. Cord (Ed.), *The Palgrave Companion to Harvard Economics* (pp. 483–495). Palgrave Macmillan.

Boskin, M., & Sheshinski, E. (1978). Optimal Redistributive Taxation When Individual Welfare Depends upon Relative Income. *The Quarterly Journal of Economics, 92*(4), 589–601.

Brady, D., & Friedman, R. (1947). Savings and the Income Distribution. In *Studies in Income and Wealth* (pp. 247–265). National Bureau of Economic Research, No.10.

Brown, T. (1952). Habit Persistence and Lags in Consumer Behaviour. *Econometrica, 20*(3), 355–371.

Corneo, G. (2002). The Efficient Side of Progressive Income Taxation. *European Economic Review, 46*(7), 1359–1368.

Drakopoulos, S. (2016). *Comparisons in Economic Thought: Economic Interdependency Reconsidered*. Routledge.

Duesenberry, J. S. (1948). Income–Consumption Relations and Their Implications. In L. Metzler (Ed.), *Income, Employment and Public Policy: Essays in Honor of Alvin H. Hansen* (pp. 54–81). W. W. Norton and Company, Inc.

Duesenberry, J. S. (1949). *Income, Saving and the Theory of Consumer Behaviour*. Harvard University Press.

Edwards, J. (2014). Consumer Power and Market Control: Exploring Consumer Behaviour in Affluent Contexts (1946–1980). *European Journal of the History of Economic Thought, 21*, 699–723.

Frank, R. (2008). Should Public Policy Respond to Positional Externalities? *Journal of Public Economics, 92*, 1777–1786.

Frantz, R. (2004). The Behavioral Economics of George Akerlof and Harvey Leibenstein. *Journal of Socio-Economics, 33*, 29–44.

Frantz, R. (2020). *The Beginnings of Behavioral Economics: Katona, Simon, and Leibenstein's X efficiency theory*. Academic Press.

Galbraith, J. K. (1958). *The Affluent Society*. Houghton Mifflin.

Hirsch, F. (1976). *Social Limits to Growth*. Harvard University Press.

Holländer, H. (2001). On the Validity of Utility Statements: Standard Theory Versus Duesenberry's. *Journal of Economic Behavior and Organization, 45*, 227–249.

Hoover, K. (2010). Microfoundational Programs. *CHOPE Working Paper*, No. 2010–01, Duke University, Center for the History of Political Economy (CHOPE), Durham, NC, pp.1–47.

Hynes, A. H. (1998). The Emergence of the Neoclassical Consumption Function: The Formative Years. 1940–1952. *Journal of the History of Economic Thought, 20*(01), 25–49.

Katona, G. (1946). Psychological Analysis of Business Decisions and Expectations. *The American Economic Review, 36*(1), 44–62.

Katona, G. (1951). *Psychological Analysis of Economic Behavior*. McGraw-Hill.

Katona, G. (1964). *The Mass Consumption Society*. McGraw-Hill.

Katona, G. (1971). Consumer Durable Spending. *Brookings Papers on Economic Activity, 1971*(1), 234–239.

Keynes, J. M. (1936). *The General Theory of Employment, Interest, and Money*, Macmillan.

King, J. (2016). Katona and Keynes. *History of Economics Review, 64*(1), 64–75.

Kosicki, G. (1990). Income Redistribution and Aggregate Consumption: Implications of the Relative Income Model. *The American Economist, 34*(1), 40–44.

Kosobud, R. (1998). Relative Income Hypothesis. In J. Eatwell, M. Milgate, & P. Newman (Eds.), *The New Palgrave: A Dictionary of Economics* (Vol. 4, pp. 134–136). Macmillan.

Leibenstein, H. (1950). Bandwagon, Snob, and Veblen Effects in the Theory of Consumers' Demand. *Quarterly Journal of Economics, 64*, 183–207.

Leibenstein, H. (1975). The Economic Theory of Fertility Decline. *Quarterly Journal of Economics, 89*, 1–31.
Leibenstein, H. (1976). *Beyond Economic Man: A New Foundation for Microeconomics*. Harvard Universities Press.
Mason, R. (2000). The Social Significance of Consumption: James Duesenberry's Contribution to Consumer Theory. *Journal of Economic Issues, 34*(3), 553–572.
McCormick, K. (1983). Duesenberry and Veblen: The Demonstration Effect Revisited. *Journal of Economic Issues, 17*, 1125–1129.
McCormick, K. (2018). James Duesenberry as a Practitioner of Behavioural Economics. *Journal of Behavioral Economics for Policy, 2*(1), 3–18.
Modigliani, F. (1949). Fluctuations in the Saving-income Ratio: A Problem in Economic Forecasting. In *Studies in Income and Wealth* (Vol. 11, pp. 369–444). National Bureau of Economic Research, Inc.
Modigliani, F. (1975). The Life-Cycle Hypothesis of Saving Twenty Years Later. In M. Parkin & A. R. Nobay (Eds.), *Contemporary Issues in Economics* (pp. 2–35). Manchester University Press.
Pollak, R. (1976). Interdependent Preferences. *American Economic Review, 66*, 745–763.
Postlewaite, A. (1998). The Social Basis of Interdependent Preferences. *European Economic Review, 42*(3–5), 779–800.
Schneider, M. (2007). The Nature, History and Significance of the Concept of Positional Goods. *History of Economics Review, 45*, 60–81.
Scitovsky, T. (1954). Two Concepts of External Economies. *Journal of Political Economy, 62*, 143–151.
Trezzini, A. (2005). The Economics of Consumption as a Social Phenomenon: A Neglected Approach to the Analysis of Consumption. *Quaderno di ricerca* n. 2, DIeS Dipartimento Innovazione e Societa` Roma, pp. 1–36.
Trezzini, A. (2012). Relative Consumption vs. permanent Income: The Crisis of the Theory of the Social Significance of Consumption. *Journal of the History of Economic Thought, 34*(3), 355–377.
Truyts, T. (2010). Social Status in Economic Theory. *Journal of Economic Surveys, 24*(1), 137–169.
Venieris, Y., & Sebold, F. (1977). *Macroeconomics: Models and Policy*. John Wiley & Sons.

CHAPTER 6

The Emergence of the Neoclassical Consumption Function

Introduction

As was seen previously, Kuznets' empirical findings provided the initial stimulus for theoretical research on aggregate consumption patterns. In the early 1950s, the emergence of life-cycle hypothesis and the permanent-income hypothesis of consumption were the 'mainstream responses' to Keynes' and Duesenberry's consumption theories. The criticism of Keynes' psychological theory was part of a more general "attack" on Keynes' approach and on standard Keynesian economics (De Vroey, 2016). For instance, Milton Friedman's (1957) anti-Keynesian offensive focused on the critique of Keynes' consumption theory and of its economic policy implications. Subsequently, Robert Lucas (1976) and others led the next wave of attack against Keynesian theory and inaugurated 'new classical macroeconomics'. In the same vein, the relative income hypothesis was rejected as a 'psychological-based' approach to consumption. Instead, Irving Fisher's (1930) intertemporal choice theory was suggested as the microeconomic foundation of aggregate consumption behaviour. Fisher's approach was grounded on the model of the rational maximising consumer, thus supplying the neoclassical alternative to consumption patterns analysis.

This chapter will start with the mainstream attitudes towards Keynes' absolute income hypothesis and Duesenberry's relative income hypothesis. It will proceed with Fisher's theory of intertemporal choice which

S. A. Drakopoulos, *The Consumption Function in Economics*,
https://doi.org/10.1007/978-3-032-15958-8_6

served as the foundation for the emerging orthodox consumption theories. It will then focus on the life-cycle and permanent-income hypotheses of consumption.

Orthodox Reactions to Keynes' and Duesenberry's Consumption Theories

Milton Friedman confronted Keynes and Keynesian economics by targeting their policy recommendations and also the Phillips curve relation that was perceived as supporting the Keynesian-based economic policies (Friedman, 1968). A few years later, Keynesian macroeconomic theory was criticised by Robert Lucas and others. Lucas attacked the methodological foundations of Keynes' theory arguing that it does not conform to the equilibrium principle consisting of (a) agents act in their own self-interest and (b) markets clear (Lucas & Sargent, 1979 1994, p. 15). Another more well-known criticism was the "Lucas critique" which states that the decision rules of Keynesian models—such as the consumption function—cannot be considered as structural in the sense of being invariant with respect to changes in government policy variables (Lucas, 1976; Sargent, 1987). According to Lucas, only deeper, 'structural models', that is, derived from the fundamentals of the economy, agents' preferences, and technological constraints, were able to provide a robust grounding for the evaluation of alternative policies. In the same vein, the new emerging macroeconomic paradigm adopted the notion of forward-looking agents with rational expectations instead of the backward-looking agents with adaptive expectations (for a detailed discussion, see De Vroey, 2016, chapter 9).

The theoretical developments regarding aggregate consumption can be explained in terms of the same conceptual framework: The life-cycle hypothesis and the permanent-income hypothesis of consumption started by employing Fisher's intertemporal choice as the microeconomic foundation of aggregate consumption, thus rejecting consumption theories involving psychological and sociological determinants, including Keynes' psychological-based approach. It can be argued that this was part of the drive to provide microfoundations to macroeconomic modelling, given that mainstream microeconomics was perceived as an established scientific branch which was free of subjective (i.e. psychological) elements (Rizvi, 1994; Bruni & Sugden, 2007; Drakopoulos & Katselidis, 2024). The following passage from Modigliani and Brumberg's seminal work on consumption is focused on Keynes' "psychological law":

> *The results of our labor basically confirm the propositions put forward by Keynes in The General Theory. At the same time, we take some satisfaction in having been able to tie this aspect of his analysis into the mainstream of economic theory by replacing his mysterious psychological law with the principle that men are disposed, as a rule and on average, to be forward-looking animals. We depart from Keynes, however, on his contention of "a greater proportion of income being saved as real income increases" … We claim instead that the proportion of income saved is essentially independent of income.* (Modigliani & Brumberg, 1954, p. 430)

It is clear that according to Modigliani and Brumberg, the main defect of Keynes' consumption analysis was the lack of microeconomic foundations (i.e. the notion of optimising individuals). Many decades later, Costas Meghir reiterates this accusation in the following statement:

> *There have been many models of consumption. An influential example is the Keynesian consumption function (Keynes, 1935) based as Keynes put it on a "basic psychological law". However his consumption function lacks any microeconomic foundations based on individual optimisation.* (Meghir, 2004, p. 297n)

Similar to Keynes' consumption theory, Duesenberry's relative income hypothesis was rejected on the same grounds, although—as was seen in the previous chapter—its initial reception by many influential economists was positive. For instance, a few years later after Modigliani's initial positive reaction that was discussed in the previous chapter, Modigliani and Brumberg claimed that their new interpretation of consumption theory was sounder and much simpler than Duesenberry's (Modigliani & Brumberg, 1954, p. 424). Modigliani and Brumberg were very critical of Duesenberry's hypothesis arguing that it contained unnecessary social and psychological elements (Mason, 2000; Pignalosa, 2025). During the same period, Milton Friedman also attacked Duesenberry's formulations by declaring that permanent income rather than relative income was the basis of consumer behaviour (Friedman, 1957). Although Friedman acknowledged some merit in Duesenberry's concept of relative income, he argued that it was basically only a biased index of relative permanent income status. Furthermore, Friedman believed that his approach was superior, since it owed nothing to sociology or to psychology, in contrast to Duesenberry's, which was full of 'subjective elements' (Friedman, 1957; see also Mason, 2000).

Much in the same way as the previous approaches involving psychological aspects and social comparisons considerations, Duesenberry's ideas never gained popularity among mainstream theorists (see also Palley, 2010). One reason might be that Duesenberry's analysis poses some fundamental questions regarding the cultural influences on economic decisions and the endogeneity of preferences, issues which were not popular for orthodox theorists. Thus, it seems that allegedly simpler explanations of consumption patterns offered by Modigliani, Brumberg, and Friedman were preferred to Duesenberry's more 'sophisticated' approach (see also Harbaugh, 1996; Cowling, 2006).

Another form of reaction against the serious consideration of relative consumption and more generally, of interdependent preferences was to diminish their theoretical importance. Given that the relative income hypothesis involves interdependent preferences, Robert Clower's stance a few years after Duesenberry's publication is indicative:

> *Interdependent preferences analysis differs but little from ordinary consumption theory; hence, while one sometimes gets different and slightly more general results in "interdependent" as compared with "independent" preference analysis, it is only in this very limited and practically unimportant sense that the two kinds of theory may be said to be at variance with one another.* (Clower, 1951, p. 178)

However, the inclusion of interdependent preferences poses serious problems for the conventional aggregate demand theory, which assumes that individual consumption behaviour is independent of the consumption of others (e.g. Pollak, 1976; Frank, 2005). Leading figures of the period like George Stigler admitted that economists refused to include in the individual's utility function the consumption of other individuals, and considered this as an important issue (Stigler, 1950). In the same vein, Oscar Morgenstern was another influential author who pointed out the serious consequences of adopting interpersonal effects on consumption (Morgenstern, 1948, p. 175). The clear implication of interdependent preferences was that aggregate demand cannot be derived from the simple summation of individual demand schedules (see also Mason, 2000; Pignalosa, 2025).

Irving Fisher's Theory of Intertemporal Choice

Rational choice theory is one of the core components of mainstream economics. Rational consumers are assumed to behave as maximising a utility function subject to the budget constraint, following the axioms of rational choice. Individual demand curves are derived from this standard model of utility maximisation. The same model is extended to include intertemporal choice, that is, the choice between consumption today versus consumption at some point in the future, which forms the basis of mainstream consumption functions. In the same way the theory of rational consumer is used to derive individual demand functions for goods and services, intertemporal maximisation is used to derive aggregate consumption functions. The savings model by Frank Ramsey (1928) is considered to be the conceptual ancestor of the optimisation approach to consumption-savings decisions. In the same period, Irving Fisher set the theoretical basis of this approach in his *Theory of Interest* (Fisher, 1930). In this framework, it is assumed that consumers are rational, forward-looking agents and choose consumption levels for the present and future so as to maximise lifetime satisfaction. Consumers' choices are subject to an intertemporal budget constraint, a measure of the total resources available for present and future consumption.

In a simple two-period model, there are two periods, period 1 (which is the present) and period 2 (which is the future). Let Y_1 and Y_2 to be income in period 1 and 2, respectively. Let C_1 and C_2 to be consumption in period 1 and period 2, respectively, and S is savings. The consumers' budget constraint in the first period is:

$$Y_1 = C_1 + S \; or \; S = Y_1 - C_1 \tag{6.1}$$

If $S > 0$ the consumer is saving, and if $S < 0$ the consumer is borrowing. Saving (borrowing) yields an interest rate (r) (costs). In the next period, consumption equals the accumulated saving (which includes the interest (r) earned on that saving), plus second-period income. The budget constraint is therefore:

$$C_2 = Y_2 + (1+r)S \; or \; C_2 = Y_2 + (1+r)(Y_1 - C_1) \tag{6.2}$$

The term $(1 + r) S$ in Eqn. (6.2) is the rate of return of savings. Rearranging terms we can write:

$$(1+r)C_1 + C_2 = Y_2 + (1+r)Y_1 \tag{6.3}$$

Dividing the above expression by $(1 + r)$, we get:

$$C_1 + \frac{C_2}{1+r} = Y_1 + \frac{Y_2}{1+r} \tag{6.4}$$

Equation (6.4) shows that the present value of lifetime consumption equals the present value of lifetime income. In other words, $1/(1 + r)$ is the relative price of future consumption in terms of current consumption: one unit of consumption today is equivalent to $1 + r$ units of consumption tomorrow. Figure 6.1 shows the optimal choice of the consumer given his/her intertemporal budget constraint.

In Fig. 6.1, the vertical axis shows consumption at period 2 (C_2) and the horizontal axis shows consumption at period 1 (C_1). The intertemporal budget constraint AB shows all combinations of C_1 and C_2 that just exhaust the consumer's resources. At point A, total available resources are equal to $Y_1 + Y_2/(1 + r)$ and are spent on present consumption. At point B the consumer postpones all consumption expenditures to period 2, and B is equal to $Y_2 + Y_1 (1 + r)$. The indifference curves (I_1, I_2, I_3) derived from the consumer's utility function demonstrate combinations of present and future consumption levels that leave the consumer equally satisfied. Higher indifference curves represent higher levels of satisfaction, and as a utility maximiser, the consumer aims to be at the highest possible indifference curve given the consumer's intertemporal budget constraint. In Fig. 6.1 the optimal point is E_o, where the slope of the budget line equals the slope of the highest possible indifference curve (I_2), and optimal consumption for the two periods are C_2^o and C_1^o. At the optimal point, the marginal rate of substitution (MRS) between present and future consumption equals the slope of the intertemporal budget constraint $(1 + r)$, (MRS $= 1 + r$). At points which are between B and E_o, the consumer has positive savings, while at points which are between E_o and A the consumer has negative savings.

Point E_o in Fig. 6.1 can change if there are changes in income (the budget line shifts) or changes in the rate of interest (the slope of the

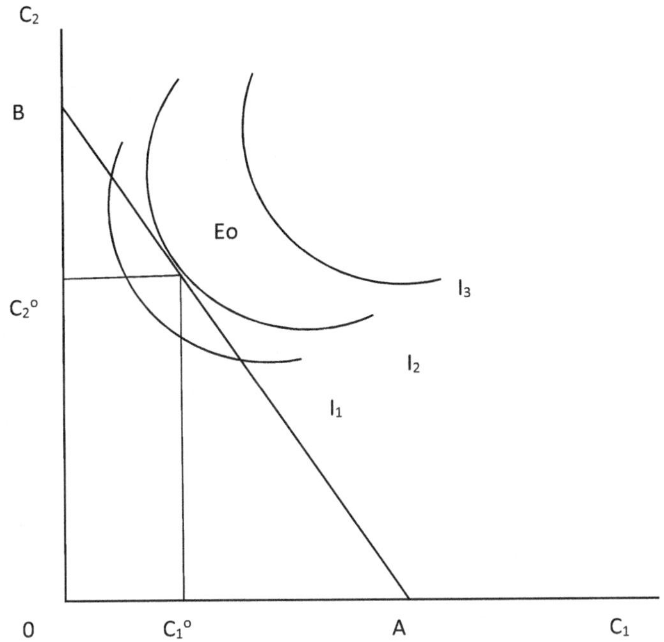

Fig. 6.1 Fisher's theory of intertemporal choice

budget line changes). Intertemporal choice theory indicates that consumption decisions depend only on the present value of lifetime income (as opposed to disposable income today). Since the consumer can borrow or lend between periods, the level of interest rate plays an important role in consumption decisions. The consumption function takes the general form:

$$C_{jt} = f\left(PW_{jt}\right) \tag{6.5}$$

In Eqn. (6.5), C_{jt} denotes the consumption expenditures of individual j at time t, and PW_{jt} is the individual's corresponding present worth. Fisher's intertemporal choice, as described above, became the microeconomic foundation of subsequent mainstream consumption theories.

The Life-Cycle Hypothesis

The life-cycle hypothesis of consumption function (LCH) was developed mainly by Franco Modigliani and Richard Brumberg in 1954 (Modigliani & Brumberg, 1954).[1] Its underlying conceptual basis is that individuals maximise their utility of consumption over their life cycle (Deaton, 2005, p. 94). The utility function can be written as:

$$U_{jt} = U_{jt}\left(C_t, C_{t+1}, C_{t+2}, \ldots, C_L\right) \tag{6.6}$$

In Eqn. (6.6), U_j is the utility of individual j, C_t is present consumption, C_{t+1} is next year's consumption, and so on, until the end of lifetime C_L. Relation (6.6) is maximised subject to the present value or worth of total resources, current and future, which will accumulate over the individual's working life. This setting implies that the individual will be able to maintain a stable pattern of consumption throughout his/her lifetime and that income from employment will behave in a fairly predictable manner (Modigliani & Brumberg, 1954).[2]

In Fig. 6.2 the horizontal axis shows time (T) while the vertical axis shows income and consumption expenditures (Y, C). Point 0 marks the beginning of the person's working life and T_2 marks the point of his/her retirement. In the early years of a person's working life and also after retirement, income is lower than consumption expenditures. For the time span T_1 to T_2 the reverse is true. As the person proceeds through life, his/her productivity increases and as a result his/her income increases up to the point of retirement T_2. From this point onwards, consumption declines but not as much as income. The hypothesis suggests that individuals take into account the profile of the stream of income during their whole productive life and pace their consumption expenditures accordingly. At the early stages of their working life and between retirement and death they have negative savings. These are balanced by the positive savings occurring

[1] For an account of the historical origins of the life-cycle hypothesis, see Martini and Spataro (2023).

[2] Margaret Reid in a 1952 paper focused on the fact that expenditure-functions are flatter for farm families than for nonfarm families. She pointed out that current income is subject to transitory shocks and spurious measurement errors, and these are likely to be more important for farm samples. This type of argument was to play an important role in the tests developed by Modigliani and Brumberg, and by Milton Friedman (Hynes, 1998, pp. 32–33).

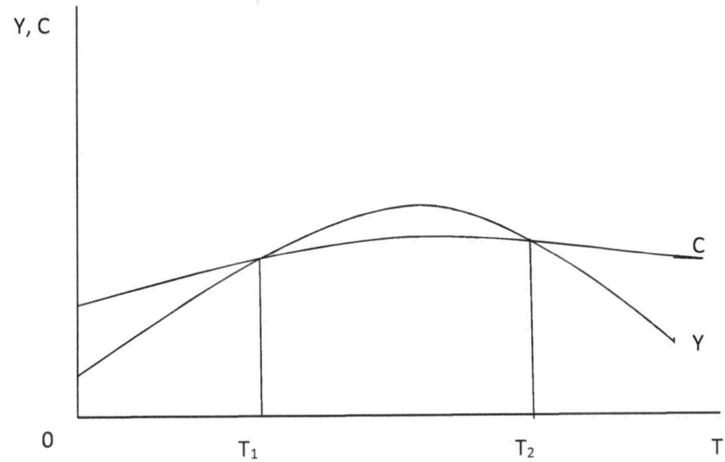

Fig. 6.2 The life-cycle hypothesis of consumption

at the time period T_1 to T_2. The above imply that the consumption function is of the general form:

$$C_t = KV_t \tag{6.7}$$

In Eqn. (6.7), C_t is the current consumption by an individual, V_t is the present value of the total resources accruing to the individual over the rest of his/her life and K is the factor of proportionality. The conceptual basis of the theory is acknowledged in a subsequent review of the theory in which Modigliani explicitly mentions that the foundation of the life-cycle hypothesis was "the received theory of consumer choice over time à la Fisher" (Modigliani, 1975, p. 5).

The present value of the total resources accruing to the individual over the rest of his/her life consumption function given by Eqn. (6.7) can also be expressed as follows:

$$V_t = \alpha x_{t-1} + Y_t + \sum_{T=1}^{n} \frac{Y_{t+T}^{e}}{(1+r_t)T} \tag{6.8}$$

Equation (6.8) shows that total resources (V_t) are made up by three components. The first component is any net worth that is carried over from the previous period (αx_{t-1}). It may take the form of inherited wealth or accumulated worth. The second term is current income Y_t, and the third term is the present value of expected future income from employment Y^e over the remainder of the individual's life time (n). Substituting the above into $C_t = KV_t$, we get:

$$C_t = K_t \alpha x_{t-1} + K_t Y_t + K_t \sum_{T=1}^{n} \frac{Y_{t+T}^e}{(1+r_t)T} \tag{6.9}$$

Equation (6.9) suggests that the discount rate (r) is an important factor in the consumption decision. Consumers are assumed to have perfect computational abilities and to be able to estimate future income correctly, implying that they do not face fundamental uncertainty in Keynes' sense. It is clear that the conceptual underpinning of this formulation is in the mainstream theory of intertemporal choice, which is based on the hypothesis of '*homo economicus*'.

The implied marginal propensity to consume of the life-cycle hypothesis can be discerned by adopting a simpler framework and assuming that real interest rate is zero. The individual divides his/her resources equally over time in order to smooth out consumption:

$$C = (W + RY)/T \tag{6.10}$$

In Eqn. (6.10), W is initial wealth, Y is annual income until retirement (assumed constant), R is the number of years until retirement, and T is lifetime in years. The same relation can be written as:

$$C = \alpha W + \beta Y \text{ with } \alpha = 1/T \text{ and } \beta = R/T \tag{6.11}$$

In Eqn. (6.11), α is the marginal propensity to consume out of wealth, and β is the marginal propensity to consume out of income.

The life-cycle hypothesis could also account for the discrepancies in empirical consumption data that was discussed previously in Chap. 4. The reasoning is the following: The life-cycle consumption function (6.11) divided by income can be written as:

$$C / Y = \alpha (W / Y) + \beta \quad (6.12)$$

Across households, income varies more than wealth, and this implies that high-income households should have a lower APC than low-income households. However, in the long run, aggregate wealth and income grow together and this results in a stable APC (Drakopoulos, 2021a). Apart from assuming perfectly rational consumers, the life-cycle consumption theory also assumes that individuals are indifferent to the form in which resources accrue. For example, a given increase in resources will have the same effect on consumption whether that increase takes the form of an increase in current income, expected income, or net worth. The life-cycle model was later developed by Modigliani jointly with Albert Ando to incorporate other factors such as the demographic structure of the population (Ando & Modigliani, 1963; see also Deaton, 2005).

Consequently, a temporary change in income is spread out over the entire lifetime so that the immediate change in consumption is small. On the other hand, a permanent change in income results in a larger change in current consumption. Thus, the MPC for an expected temporary change in income will be much smaller than that for an expected permanent change in income (Jappelli & Pistaferri, 2014). It is clear that the consumer's income plays a much smaller role in consumption decisions than in Keynes' and Duesenberry's theories. For instance, the life-cycle model predicts a smaller impact of tax cuts than the Keynesian consumption function since tax cuts are smoothed and spent over an individual's entire remaining lifespan (Bunting, 2001; Drakopoulos, 2021b).

An obvious prediction of the life-cycle model is that individuals should save enough before retirement in order to maintain consumption levels after retirement. However, if consumers enter retirement with inadequate savings, they must cut their consumption level, contrary to the life-cycle theory (Hamermesh, 1984; see also Attanasio & Weber, 2010). Further, one of the basic assumptions of life-cycle theory is the switching of assets. However and as many critics have suggested, asset switching is not a costless transaction (e.g. Deaton, 1992). Moreover, the life-cycle theory ignores imperfections in capital markets, which impose a limit on the amount an individual can borrow (liquidity constraint). Liquidity constraints affect the ability of households to transfer resources across time periods (Jappelli & Pistaferri, 2017, pp. 82–93). Other criticisms involve the role of future income uncertainty which undermines the core assumption of optimising consumers (e.g. Carroll, 1997; Deaton, 2005). Finally, another line of criticism has to do with the notion of expected income, which is part of the individual's total resources. This variable is not directly observable and its value has to be forecast, something that poses difficulties for the empirical testing of the theory (see Deaton, 1992; Pemberton, 1997).

The Permanent-Income Hypothesis

The main attempt to criticise Keynes' approach to consumption was made by Milton Friedman with his permanent-income hypothesis (PIH).[3] In the process of defining the consumption function, Friedman (1957) rejects Keynes' use of current income as the determinant of consumption expenditure, based on the assumption of forward-looking consumers. Friedman argued that Fisher's model is the "pure theory of consumer behavior" and that it makes the wealth approach a sounder account than that of Keynes' (Friedman, 1957, p. 6). He started with an analysis of individual decision-making, yielding an intertemporal utility-maximising equation that he described as 'a cornerstone' of his permanent-income theory of the consumption function (Friedman, 1957, p. 14). In fact, the permanent-income hypothesis is a special case of an intertemporal optimisation model of consumer behaviour, where agents maximise the sum of their expected utility subject to a life-time budget constraint (Meghir, 2004). Consumers use their savings (or borrow) in an attempt to smooth consumption between good and bad years. It follows that current income differs from permanent income:

$$Y_t = Y^P + Y^T \tag{6.13}$$

In Eqn. (6.13), Y_t is current income at time t, Y^P is permanent income projected at time t, and Y^T is transitory (or unexpected changes in) income. The transitory component has an expected value of zero reflecting the notion that over time transitory gains are offset by future transitory losses and vice versa. Thus, in the long-run, observed levels of income (Y) are equal to permanent income (Y^P) (Friedman, 1957; see also Meghir, 2004).

[3] Jennifer Burns (2022) provides an alternate history of Milton Friedman's consumption function, spotlighting the contributions of his collaborators Margaret Reid, Dorothy Brady, and Rose Friedman.

Friedman also assumed that permanent income is an average of income over the last several years. Income would have to increase for several years continuously before people would expect permanent income to increase. In other words, and assuming adaptive expectations, consumers correct their previous estimates of permanent income by the amount of deviation of current income from previous period estimated permanent income (Friedman, 1957; see also Chao, 2003). Further, Ando and Modigliani (1963) modified Friedman's theory by incorporating the prior insight of Modigliani and Brumberg (1954) that because consumers are not infinitely lived, the aggregate pattern of consumption over the life-cycle has to be taken into account when considering the impact of permanent income on consumption (Foster, 2021, p. 776).

In the same way as income, consumption (C) is divided into permanent consumption, C^P, and transitory consumption, C^T. Thus:

$$C_t = C^P + C^T \tag{6.14}$$

Just like transitory income, transitory consumption is regarded as temporary. Friedman assumes that permanent consumption is a constant proportion of permanent income, while permanent and transitory consumption may be interpreted as 'planned' and 'unplanned' consumption, respectively. Based on Friedman's assumption that Y^T is uncorrelated to C, any unforeseen increment in income does not result in unplanned consumption. Friedman justifies this premise by pointing out that even if income is other than expected, the consumer would tend to stick to his/her consumption plan, but adjust his/her asset holdings. The key point is that the consumption plan does not depend on the transitory components (Friedman, 1957; for a detailed discussion, see Chao, 2003 and Meghir, 2004).

Given the above, Friedman's permanent-income consumption function is:

$$C^P = k(r,z)Y^P \tag{6.15}$$

In Eqn. (6.15), $k(r, z)$ is the average (or marginal) propensity to consume out of permanent income which depends on the rate of interest (r) and on taste shifter variables (z). Friedman's reconciliation of the empirical findings on consumption was based on the differences in consumption behaviour of different income groups. Over the long run, income variation is due mainly, if not solely, to variation in permanent income, which in addition to equality between APC and MPC implies a stable and less than unity APC (Chao, 2003; Meghir, 2004). The following figure illustrates Friedman's main argument.

In Fig. 6.3, the horizontal axis shows income (Y) while the vertical axis shows consumption (C). The figure shows that permanent consumption function is the long-run consumption function curve C_{LR} ($C_{LR} = kY^P$). The long-run consumption function indicates the proportional relationship between consumption and implies that APC is constant and is equal to MPC. C_{SR1} and C_{SR2} are short-run consumption function curves and are flatter compared to the long-run consumption function curve (this implies that in the short-run MPC < APC). In the short-run consumption function curves, measured income includes both permanent and transitory components. If there is an increase in income in the short-run, the consumer will move from E_0 to E_1 if he/she does not expect the rise in income to be permanent. Thus, APC falls as income increases. But if the increase in income level becomes permanent, the consumer will also increase his/her consumption permanently. The short-run consumption function will shift upwards from C_{SR1} to C_{SR2} and intersect the long-run consumption function at point E_2 with higher income level at Y_2.

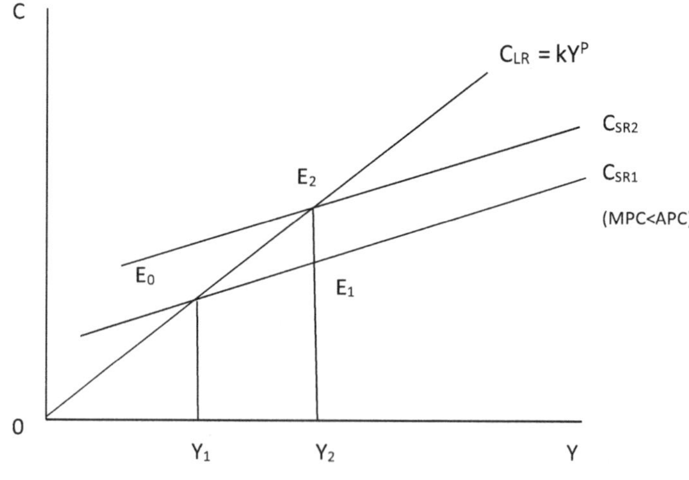

Fig. 6.3 Permanent-income hypothesis

If consumption is proportional to permanent income, the power of tax-induced changes in aggregate demand is reduced. In terms of policy implications, the Keynesian case for activist fiscal policy is further weakened (Snowdon & Vane, 2005, p. 195). In Friedman's words:

> *current consumption is adapted to some measure of longer-run income status, ... a much larger part of current income is interpreted as autonomous and a much smaller part as dependent on current income. ... The result is a smaller investment multiplier, and an inherently cyclically more stable system.* (Friedman, 1957, p. 238)

In general, Friedman's permanent income hypothesis offered another way of explaining the conflicting results of early empirical studies on consumption. It distinguished between a short-run and a long-run consumption function. The long-run function was essentially a proportional relation, while the short-run function was a non-proportional one. Contrary to Keynes' and Duesenberry's consumption theories, the interest rate plays the important role of converting future resources to present ones and therefore constitutes an important determinant of consumption in both life-cycle and permanent-income theories (Attanasio & Weber, 2010). In addition, the smoothed consumption path as PIH postulates can be realised only under the assumption of perfect capital markets, meaning that frictions in borrowing and lending do not hinder the optimisation process (Flemming, 1973; see also Galbacs, 2015, pp. 228–229). The criticisms of the life-cycle theory involving the notions of liquidity constraints, uncertainty about future income, and of the observability and measurability of permanent income also apply to Friedman's theory (Bird & Bodkin, 1965; Heller & Starr, 1979; Jappelli & Pistaferri, 2017, pp. 82–93).[4]

Concluding Comments

Following the strong criticism by mainstream economists, Keynes' 'psychological' approach to consumption, and Duesenberry's relative consumption hypothesis, eventually fell out of favour. They were replaced by the life-cycle hypothesis and the permanent-income hypothesis as part of

[4] For an early heterodox critique of Life-Cycle and Permanent-Income theories, see Green (1984).

a wider paradigm shift in macroeconomic theory (De Vroey, 2016). These two theories started by employing Fisher's intertemporal choice as the microeconomic foundation of aggregate consumption, thus rejecting Keynes' psychological-based approach to consumption. It is indicative that Modigliani, Brumberg, and Friedman explicitly argued for the need to utilise the 'pure' or 'accepted' theory of consumer choice in aggregate consumption, and they devoted considerable effort to this task. They were arguing that the theory of consumer choice had "received inadequate attention" and that its "implications have been incompletely recognized" (Modigliani & Brumberg, 1954, pp. 390–397; Friedman, 1957, pp. 7–19; see also Bunting, 2001, p. 157).

The life-cycle hypothesis and the permanent-income hypothesis with the core assumptions of utility maximising and forward-looking agents eventually became established in economics orthodoxy. They also became the foundation for the subsequent emergence of consumption theories involving agents with rational expectations, as will be seen in the next chapter. However, Keynes' and Duesenberry's approaches did not disappear. Heterodox economists and heterodox schools of thought employed some of their key elements in their theoretical constructs as will be discussed in Chap. 8.

References

Ando, A., & Modigliani, F. (1963). The 'Life-Cycle' Hypothesis of Saving: Aggregate Implications and Tests. *American Economic Review, 53*, 55–84.

Attanasio, O., & Weber, G. (2010). Consumption and Saving: Models of Intertemporal Allocation and Their Implications for Public Policy. *Journal of Economic Literature, 48*(3), 693–751.

Bird, R., & Bodkin, R. (1965). The National Service Life Insurance Dividends of 1950 and Consumption–a Further Test of the 'strict' Permanent Income Hypothesis. *Journal of Political Economy, 73*(5), 499–515.

Bruni, L., & Sugden, R. (2007). The Road Not Taken: How Psychology was Removed from Economics, and How it Might be Brought Back. *The Economic Journal, 117*, 146–173.

Bunting, D. (2001). Keynes's Law and Its Critics. *Journal of Post Keynesian Economics, 24*, 149–163.

Burns, J. (2022). Hidden Figures: A New History of the Permanent Income Hypothesis. *History of Political Economy, 54*(S1), 43–68.

Carroll, C. (1997). Buffer-stock Saving and the Life-cycle/Permanent Income Hypothesis. *Quarterly Journal of Economics, 112*(1), 1–55.

Chao, H.-K. (2003). Milton Friedman and the Emergence of the Permanent Income Hypothesis. *History of Political Economy, 35*(1), 77–104.

Clower, R. (1951). Professor Duesenberry and Traditional Theory. *Review of Economic Studies, 19*, 165–178.

Cowling, K. (2006). Prosperity, Depression and Modern Capitalism. *Kyklos, 59*, 369–381.

De Vroey, M. (2016). *A History of Macroeconomics from Keynes to Lucas and Beyond*. Cambridge University Press.

Deaton, A. (1992). *Macroeconomics and Consumption*. Oxford University Press.

Deaton, A. (2005). Franco Modigliani and the Life-Cycle Theory of Consumption. *BNL Quarterly Review LVIII, 233–234*, 91–107.

Drakopoulos, S. (2021a). Theories of Consumption. In L.-P. Rochon & S. Rosi (Eds.), *An introduction to Macroeconomics* (pp. 233–267). Edward Elgar.

Drakopoulos, S. (2021b). The Marginalization of Absolute and Relative Income Hypotheses of Consumption and the Role of Fiscal Policy. *The European Journal of the History of Economic Thought, 28*(6), 965–984.

Drakopoulos, S., & Katselidis, I. (2024). *Economics and Psychology: An Uneasy History*. Routledge.

Fisher, I. (1930). *The Theory of Interest*. Macmillan.

Flemming, J. (1973). The Consumption Function When Capital Markets are Imperfect–the Permanent Income Hypothesis Reconsidered. *Oxford Economic Papers, 25*(2), 160–172.

Foster, J. (2021). The US Consumption Function: A New Perspective. *Journal of Evolutionary Economics, 31*, 773–798.

Frank, R. (2005). Positional Externalities Cause Large and Preventable Welfare Losses. *American Economic Review, 95*(2), 137–141.

Friedman, M. (1957). *The Consumption Function*. Princeton University Press.

Friedman, M. (1968). The Role of Monetary Policy. *American Economic Review, 58*, 1–17.

Galbacs, P. (2015). *The Theory of New Classical Macroeconomics: A Positive Critique*. Springer.

Green, F. (1984). A Critique of the Neo-Fisherian Consumption Function. *Review of Radical Political Economics, 16*(2–3), 95–114.

Hamermesh, D. (1984). Consumption during Retirement: The Missing Link in the Life Cycle. *Review of Economics and Statistics, 66*(1), 1–7.

Harbaugh, R. (1996). Falling Beyond the Joneses: Relative Consumption and the Growth-Savings Paradox. *Economics Letters, 53*, 297–304.

Heller, W., & Starr, R. (1979). Capital Market Imperfection, the Consumption Function, and the Effectiveness of Fiscal Policy. *Quarterly Journal of Economics, 93*(3), 455–463.

Hynes, A. H. (1998). The Emergence of the Neoclassical Consumption Function: The Formative Years. 1940–1952. *Journal of the History of Economic Thought, 20*(01), 25–49.

Jappelli, T., & Pistaferri, L. (2014). Fiscal Policy and MPC Heterogeneity. *American Economic Journal: Macroeconomics, 6*(4), 107–136.

Jappelli, T., & Pistaferri, L. (2017). *The Economics of Consumption: Theory and Evidence*. Oxford University Press.

Lucas, R. ([1976] 1981). Econometric Policy Evaluation: A Critique. reprinted in *Studies in Business Cycle Theory.* Cambridge (Mass.): The M.I.T. Press, pp. 104–130.

Lucas, R., & Sargent, T. (1979.] (1994)). After Keynesian Macroeconomics. In P. Miller (Ed.), *The Rational Expectations Revolution: Readings from the Front Line* (pp. 5–30). The M.I.T. Press.

Martini, A., & Spataro, L. (2023). At the Origins of the Life Cycle Hypothesis of Franco Modigliani and Richard Brumberg: An Attempt at Analysis. *The European Journal of the History of Economic Thought, 31*(1), 77–110.

Mason, R. (2000). The Social Significance of Consumption: James Duesenberry's Contribution to Consumer Theory. *Journal of Economic Issues, 34*(3), 553–572.

Meghir, C. (2004). A Retrospective on Friedman's Theory of Permanent Income. *The Economic Journal, 114*(496), F293–F306.

Modigliani, F. (1975). The Life-Cycle Hypothesis of Saving Twenty Years Later. In M. Parkin & A. R. Nobay (Eds.), *Contemporary Issues in Economics* (pp. 2–35). Manchester University Press.

Modigliani, F., & Brumberg, R. (1954). Utility Analysis and the Consumption Function: An Interpretation of Cross-Section Data. In K. K. Kurihara (Ed.), *Post-Keynesian Economics* (pp. 388–436). Rutgers University Press.

Morgenstern, O. (1948). Demand Theory Reconsidered. *Quarterly Journal of Economics, 62*, 165–201.

Palley, T. (2010). Relative Permanent Income Theory of Consumption: A Synthetic Keynes- Duesenberry- Friedman Model. *Review of Political Economy, 22*(1), 41–56.

Pemberton, J. (1997). The Empirical Failure of the Life Cycle Model with Perfect Capital Markets. *Oxford Economic Papers, 49*(2), 129–151.

Pignalosa, D. (2025). Consumption as a Social Phenomenon in the Modern Theory of Intertemporal Choice. *Review of Political Economy, 37*(2), 543–563.

Pollak, R. (1976). Interdependent Preferences. *American Economic Review, 66*, 745–763.

Ramsey, F. (1928). A Mathematical Theory of Saving. *Economic Journal, 38*(152), 543–559.

Reid, M. (1952). Effect of Income Concept Upon Expenditure Curves of Farm Families. *Studies in Income and Wealth,* 15, National Bureau of Economic Research, New York.

Rizvi, S. (1994). The Microfoundations Project in General Equilibrium Theory. *Cambridge Journal of Economics, 18*(4), 357–377.

Sargent, T. (1987). *"Lucas's Critique". Macroeconomic Theory* (2nd ed.). Academic Press.

Snowdon, B., & Vane, H. (2005). *Modern Macroeconomics: Its Origins, Development and Current State*. Edward Elgar.

Stigler, G. (1950). The Development of Utility Theory. II. *Journal of Political Economy, 58*, 373–396.

CHAPTER 7

Current Status of the Mainstream Consumption Functions

Introduction

As was observed in the previous chapter, the first Neoclassical consumption theories to appear—the LCH and PIH hypotheses—employed Fisher's intertemporal choice as the microeconomic foundation of aggregate consumption. The introduction of utility maximisers, forward-looking agents by both life-cycle and permanent-income hypothesis into consumption theory, gave them increasing acceptance in mainstream macroeconomic theory (Laidler, 2010). The important consequence was the gradual abandonment of Keynes' psychological-based approach to consumption. The Neoclassical consumption was part of the drive to provide microfoundations to macroeconomic modelling, given the perceived high scientific status of mainstream microeconomics. The aim to unify economic theory with the eventual disappearance of the micro-macro demarcation was another factor towards microfoundations (Taylor, 2004). Moreover, orthodox microeconomics, and especially the theory of rational choice, was considered to be entirely free of subjective or psychological underpinnings (Rizvi, 1994; King, 2012). This went in tandem with the methodological position of isolating economics from other social disciplines such as psychology, a position still discernable today (Bruni & Sugden, 2007; Goodwin, 2016; Drakopoulos & Katselidis, 2019).

The effort to provide neoclassical microfoundations to consumption function intensified. As a result, subsequent formulations of consumption

S. A. Drakopoulos, *The Consumption Function in Economics*,
https://doi.org/10.1007/978-3-032-15958-8_7

were essentially extensions of the life-cycle and of the permanent-income theories (for a general review, see Jappelli & Pistaferri, 2017). The new element was the assumption of agents characterised by rational expectations: people use all available information to forecast future variables like income. One indicative example of such theories is Robert Hall's (1978) random walk theory of consumption. The other major change was the introduction of the representative agent, which is used in most current mainstream macroeconomic modelling. The constrained utility-maximiser model of individual behaviour was, and still is, perceived as a solid theoretical basis for its extension to macroeconomics. The rise of the representative agent was almost parallel to the gradual emergence of the new neoclassical synthesis (Goodfriend & King, 1997; Hoover, 2012). Nowadays, it is better known as dynamic stochastic general equilibrium (DSGE) theory.

This chapter will start with a discussion of the random-walk theory of consumption and rational expectations. There will also be a discussion of the empirical testing of the random walk theories and of their modifications in view of their empirical shortcomings. It will continue with a description of the contemporary general equilibrium macroeconometric models (e.g. DSGE) and the consumption function. Variations of the above models with reference to consumption function such as Heterogeneous Agent New Keynesian (HANK) and Two-Agents New Keynesian (TANK) models will also be discussed.

Rational Expectations and Random Walk Theory of Consumption

In the 1970s, the theories by Modigliani, Brumberg, and Friedman were revised with the introduction of the key assumption of rational expectations. Given the rise of rational expectations theory, Friedman's assumption of adaptive expectations did not fit the emerging conceptual framework (Lucas, 1972; Deaton, 1992; Galbacs, 2015). John Muth formulated the rational expectations hypothesis in the context of microeconomics, but it had a huge impact on subsequent orthodox macroeconomic theory (Muth, 1961). More specifically, Robert Hall's (1978) random walk theory of consumption proposed to use the first-order conditions of the intertemporal optimisation problem faced by the consumer—the Euler equation—to derive a set of conditions suitable for empirical verification (Pignalosa, 2021).[1] As the title of his main article indicated, Hall examined the stochastic implications of the Life Cycle-Permanent Income Hypothesis. The basic argument was that if expectations concerning income are fully rational, in the sense of taking into account all available information about the future, then consumption should not depend on a weighted average of past income but will, instead, follow a random walk (Hall, 1978). Based on the presentation by Pignalosa (2021, pp. 4–6), the analytical framework is an individual who maximises lifetime utility subject to an intertemporal budget constraint and a terminal condition on wealth. The optimisation problem is:

$$[\![E_t\left[\sum_{j=0}^{T-t}\beta^{t+j}u\left(C_{t+j}\right)\right] \tag{7.1}$$

s.t.

$$A_{t+1} = \left(A_t + Y_t - C_t\right)\left(1+r\right)$$
$$A_t \geq 0$$

where β=1/1+δ.

In the optimisation problem described by 7.1, β is the discount factor, which is positive and smaller than unity because the rate of time preference, δ, is positive; C_t is the level of consumption in period t, u() is the within-period utility function, which is continuous, increasing, and strictly concave; $[\![E_t$ is the expectations operator that takes expectations of variables conditional on the information available at time t; A_t is wealth at time t and r is the rate of interest, assumed to be constant over time. The first order conditions of the above problem supply the Euler equation for consumption:

$$u'\left(C_t\right) = \frac{1+r}{1+\delta}[\![E_t\left[u'\left(C_{t+1}\right)\right] \tag{7.2}$$

[1]The formal statement of Hall's result relied on the mathematical optimality condition known as the Euler equation. Tests of the kind Hall proposed became known as Euler equation tests (Carroll, 2001, p. 36).

Equation 7.2 is usually called the Euler equation. It can be viewed as the standard optimality condition equating marginal costs and marginal benefits. The equation demonstrates that the marginal utility cost of foregoing one unit of consumption at time t is equal to the marginal utility benefit from investing that unit at time t and consuming the proceeds at time t + 1 (for a detailed analysis, see Deaton, 1992; Pignalosa, 2021, pp. 4–6).

The crucial implication of the Euler equation was that a change in income or wealth that was anticipated has already been factored into expected permanent income, so that it will not change consumption. Consequently, only unanticipated changes in income or wealth that change expected permanent income will change consumption (Foster, 2021). In the rational expectations framework, agents anticipate the future and therefore make all the required adjustments in the current period. The equation for future consumption is:

$$C_{t+1} = C_t + Q_{t+1} \tag{7.3}$$

In Eq. (7.3), Q_{t+1} is a rational expectations error that cannot be predicted with any information known at time *t*. All future information is reflected in current consumption, C_t. Thus, consumption is a random walk, as changes over time are unforeseeable (for details, see Carroll, 2001). In general, Hall's model predicts that, in each period, current consumption is the same as in the previous period, unless new information about lifetime resources leads the consumer to adjust her/his consumption plan (Pignalosa, 2025).

Empirical Testing and Modifications of the Euler Equation

There were many subsequent empirical papers attempting to test Hall's model of consumption. A considerable number of these papers pointed to some 'consumption puzzles' with the clear implication that the model might be inadequate to explain aggregate consumption behaviour. For instance, an early paper by Flavin (1981) indicated that contrary to Hall's core suggestions, aggregate consumption does in fact depend on anticipated income changes. It became known as the 'excess sensitivity of consumption puzzle' (see also Campbell & Mankiw, 1989). Other puzzles include the 'retirement consumption puzzle', which means that consumers retire with inadequate savings (i.e. Hamermesh, 1984), and the 'wealth decumulation puzzle' referring to the finding that elderly consumers either continue to save in retirement or decumulate their wealth much more slowly than would be predicted by the intertemporal maximisation model (i.e. Bernheim, 1987). The 'equity premium puzzle' is another problem for the standard model referring to its inability to explain household portfolio choices (Siegel & Thaler, 1997; Carroll, 2001).

The general impression regarding the empirical testing of Hall's formulation was rather disappointing, given that the empirical evidence indicated a lack of smoothing across stages of life. In particular, much of the evidence pointed to rejections of the life-cycle model that took the form of 'excess sensitivity' of consumption to income (for a review, see Attanasio & Weber, 2010). It is indicative that many influential macroeconomists openly admit the empirical failure of the Euler consumption. Summarising the results of a survey of macroeconomists, Oliver Blanchard finds that "the foundations of the consumption Euler equation have no empirical support" (Blanchard, 2025, p. 24). Further, studies have found that consumption tracks income during the life-cycle suggesting that current income exerts a larger influence on consumption than the theory would imply, thereby providing support for the Keynesian approach to explaining consumption behaviour (Carroll & Summers, 1991; Pignalosa, 2021, p. 12).

As a reaction to the empirical failures and puzzles arising from Hall's consumption framework, many specialists in the following decades started to modify the original model in the attempt to make it capable of explaining the data (García et al., 2023). Binding liquidity constraints, 'rule of thumb' consumers, and the related notion of 'hand-to mouth' consumers, were some of the main modifications. Binding liquidity constraints relax the assumption of perfect credit markets, thus imposing a limit to borrowing possibilities by consumers (e.g. Zeldes, 1989; Campbell & Mankiw, 1990). The presence of a binding liquidity constraint means that the consumer is at a kink of the intertemporal budget constraint, implying a problem for the tangency requirement of the ratio of marginal utilities and intertemporal prices (Attanasio & Weber, 2010, p. 712). The situation can also be depicted in the following Fig. 7.1 in terms of Fisher's intertemporal choice model that was seen in the previous chapter (Fig. 6.1).

In Fig. 7.1, the vertical axis shows consumption at period 2 (C_2) and the horizontal axis shows consumption at period 1 (C_1). In the absence of

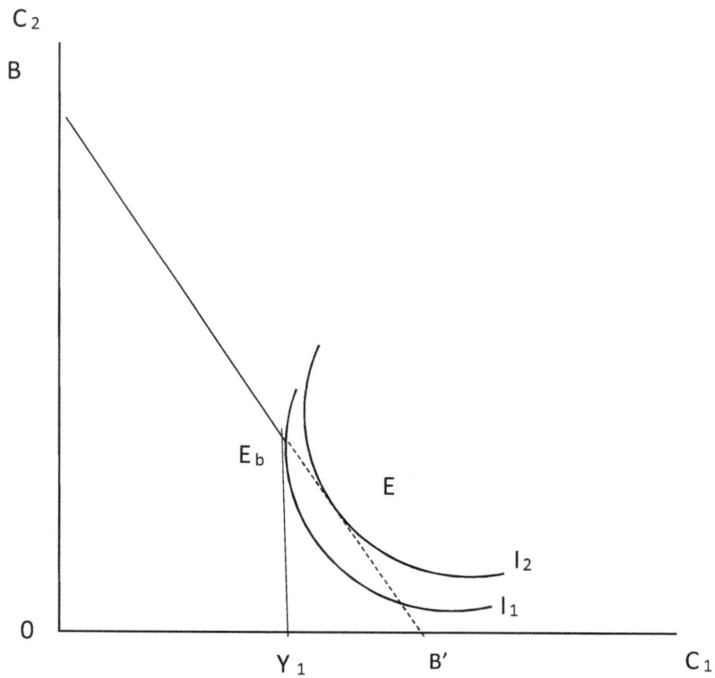

Fig. 7.1 Consumer optimisation when the borrowing constraint is binding

binding borrowing constraint the intertemporal budget constraint is BB' and shows all combinations of C_1 and C_2 that just exhaust the consumer's resources. In this case, the consumer optimal choice is at point E, where the slope of the indifference curve I_2 derived from the consumer's utility function equals the slope of the intertemporal budget constraint. However, in the presence of binding borrowing constraint, the intertemporal budget constraint is BE_bY_1. In this case, the consumer can only achieve point E_b (with $C_1 = Y_1$) which is on a lower indifference curve I_1, thus leading to a suboptimal choice. It is clear that for consumers who are not able to borrow, consumption depends only on current income, implying that the Keynesian analysis is more relevant than Fisher's two-period model.

The rule of thumb consumers consume a fixed proportion of their disposable income (e.g. Campbell & Mankiw, 1991). Further, empirical studies of wealth accumulation and consumption patterns indicate the relevance of the rule of thumb behaviour (Bernheim et al., 2001; see also Winter et al., 2012). Hand-to-mouth consumers are consumers who simply consume their current income, regardless of the reason, and their behaviour could be the result of a rule of thumb effect (e.g. Attanasio et al., 2020). These assumptions can explain that a large fraction of the population is highly sensitive to income changes or the 'excess sensitivity' seen above, which is a fundamental violation of the basic model (Attanasio & Weber, 2010, pp. 711–712).

Consumption and DSGE Models

Currently, the consumption Euler equation is not only the principal component of the theory of intertemporal choice, but also a basic building block of dynamic general equilibrium models (DSGE), and hence one of the most popular tools of mainstream macroeconomic analysis (Hendry & Muellbauer, 2018; Pignalosa, 2021).[2] In fact, since the mid-2000s, most general equilibrium models have had a DSGE-like structure (Blanchard, 2025). The rational expectations approach combined with Friedman's notion of permanent-income hypothesis are in the hard core of contemporary general equilibrium macroeconometric models (Muellbauer, 2016). The canonical rational expectations permanent income (REPIH) consumption function is given as:

$$c_t = rA_{t-1} + y_t^P \tag{7.4}$$

In Eq. 7.4, consumption, c_t, is equal to property income defined as the real rate of return, r, times last period's real wealth, A, plus permanent non-property income y^P. The symbol y^P is defined as that constant level of real non-property income which, sustained over the life cycle, has the same present value as the income stream actually expected, where future incomes are discounted at the real rate of return. Consequently, aggregate behaviour of households is assumed to be the same as that of an average household, the simplest case of a representative agent (Muellbauer, 2016).

[2] The Dynamic Stochastic General Equilibrium (DSGE) and the US Federal Reserve's (FRB) model—a more policy-oriented and less microfounded model—are the dominant models used by Central Banks (Woodford, 2009; Muellbauer, 2016; Hendry & Muellbauer, 2018).

In most DSGE models, the consumption function consists of a representative agent maximising his/her utility over an infinite lifetime without borrowing constraints. In addition, agents form their expectations about the future in a rational way (Meeusen, 2011; Stiglitz, 2018). In the words of Oliver Blanchard: "Aggregate demand is derived as consumption demand by infinitely lived and foresighted consumers" (Blanchard, 2016, p. 1).

In the form of the representative agent modelling, the constrained utility-maximiser model of individual behaviour was, and still is, perceived as a solid theoretical basis for its extension to macroeconomics. The vast majority of the DSGE models share the common features of a commitment to microfoundations and an acceptance that all behaviour is based on expected utility-maximisation (Hands, 2017, p. 1687; see also King, 2012). In spite of its wide usage in mainstream macroeconomics, the DSGE theory has been criticised by many prominent macroeconomic theorists (for summaries, see Kirman, 1992; Hartley, 1997; Hands, 2017; Marchionatti & Sella, 2017, and the discussion on Chap. 9).

Alternatives to the Representative Agent Model

Apart from the criticism of the DSGE approach, the financial crisis of 2008 was also a stimulus for macroeconomists to search for alternative formulations including the assumptions concerning agents, and in particular, the notion of representative agent.[3] The origin of the alternative agent modelling was the work of Campbell and Mankiw (1989), who proposed a simple two-agent framework with unconstrained and hand-to-mouth households, thus departing from the representative household formalism dominant at that time. Subsequent works such as Gali et al. (2007) and Bilbiie (2008) employed the two-agent framework into the New Keynesian model, establishing the so-called two-agent New Keynesian (TANK) models. More recent contributions include Bilbiie (2020), and Cantore and Freund (2021), among others. Apart from standard unconstraint agents who can freely borrow and save, TANK models include hand-to-mouth agents, who are shut out of financial markets and are

[3] It is also very interesting that recently some Central Banks (such as the ECB) have admitted the serious weaknesses of the DSGE framework, and of its assumptions regarding agent behaviour as foundations for their models. This happened after the financial crisis and especially after the COVID pandemic (e.g. Ciccarelli et al., 2024).

unable to borrow and lend. Given their behaviour, hand-to-mouth agents or households just consume their disposable income each period. As a consequence, it seems that these models can explain the high marginal propensities to consume in the data, and the associated Keynesian multiplier and fiscal policy effects (Galí et al., 2007; Bilbiie, 2020).

In contrast to the orthodox representative agent New Keynesian (RANK) models, the TANK models were the first ones to introduce heterogeneous agents in standard macroeconomic modelling. More recently, a class of models, often referred to as HANK (for Heterogeneous Agent New Keynesian) have emerged as another alternative to the representative agent paradigm (Bilbiie, 2020). Heterogeneity in those models is usually introduced by assuming that agents/households are subject to non-insurable idiosyncratic income shocks that cannot be insured against due to incomplete financial markets and are subject to some form of a borrowing constraint. The combination of uninsurable income shocks and a borrowing constraint makes the distribution of household wealth matter. Some households will always be at the borrowing constraint, behaving like the hand-to-mouth households in the TANK model. However, one of the key differences from the TANK models was that there will be time variation in how many households are constrained, implying a continuum of heterogeneous households with different incomes and asset positions. Most HANK formulations followed the insights of an influential paper by Kaplan et al., 2018 (see also Debortoli & Galí, 2024).

Contrary to the standard RANK models, the innovative aspect of most of TANK and HANK models is that their policy implications resemble the "old" Keynesian ones. In particular, key mechanisms of many of those models point to the revival of concepts such as 'The Keynesian cross', the marginal propensity to consume (MPC), and monetary and fiscal multipliers (e.g. Kaplan et al., 2018; Bilbiie, 2020; Auclert et al., 2024). For instance, Florin Bilbiie states:

> *Much like the old Keynesian cross when the marginal propensity to consume MPC increases, my model implies a steeper planned-expenditure curve: monetary and fiscal multipliers and large general-equilibrium feedback effects arise when we add households with unit MPC out of <u>their own</u> income so that <u>aggregate</u> MPC increases.* (Bilbiie, 2020, p. 91, emphasis in the original)

In other words, the introduction of heterogeneous agents in New Keynesian models makes the basic conclusions of standard Keynesian analysis much more relevant after a long period of theoretical undermining by Neoclassical and New Keynesian approaches.[4] It should be noted though, that most heterogeneous agents models still assume the existence of an Euler equation and optimising behaviour for at least some of the agents.

It should also be mentioned that a relatively recent alternative to the standard representative agent construction is the Agent-Based Models (ABM). Agent-based modelling is a novel computational methodology for representing the behaviour of individuals in order to study social phenomena. Having interdisciplinary origins, the ABM approach is increasingly popular in economics and finance, and it is part of the attempt to relax conventional assumptions in economic models. One interesting characteristic of this literature is the attempt to move beyond the representative agent, to include more agents and to make them heterogeneous (Axtell & Farmer, 2025). Regarding macroeconomics, there are a number of works examining how interactions between agents could provide new insights for economic policy (e.g. Aoki, 2001; for a review see Axtell & Farmer, 2025).

Habit Formation, Catching Up, and Keeping Up with the Joneses

Apart from heterogeneous agents, habit-formation is another hypothesis that has been introduced in the representative agent macroeconomics literature (Carroll et al., 2020). In the context of consumption analysis, the assumption of habit-forming preferences imply utility to depend on how current consumption compares to one's own consumption in the past. As a consequence, utility is no longer time separable because the choice of a consumption level today affects the habit stock, which in turn affects next period's and all future periods' utility, so that the marginal utility of current consumption depends on future consumption (Pignalosa, 2025). The inclusion of habit-formation in standard models implies that they can provide an explanation of the excess smoothness of consumption (e.g. Kiley, 2010). As Daria Pignalosa states:

[4] For empirical evidence of agent/household heterogeneity regarding accumulation behaviour in the Euro Area countries, see Arrondel et al. (2014).

> *Habit-forming individuals choose a steeper consumption profile over time because they benefit not only from consumption levels but also from consumption growth. In addition, because of their stronger aversion to consumption declines, habit-forming consumers smooth consumption changes over and above the smoothing implied by the life cycle-permanent income hypothesis with time-separable preferences.* (Pignalosa, 2025, p. 552)

Further, the presence of habits has also been shown to have important implications for the responsiveness of tax and monetary policy, and for the asset pricing models such as the equity premium puzzle (e.g. Fuhrer, 2000; Bernasconi et al., 2020).

Similar to habit formation, there is a strand of literature that employs the notions of 'catching up with the Joneses', or 'keeping up with the Joneses' (for a discussion, see Pignalosa, 2025). In terms of agents, these two notions are examples of interdependent or social preferences: individual preferences and tastes are constantly influenced by the preferences and actions of other individuals.[5] It is clear that interdependent preferences violate one of the core assumptions of orthodox economic theory, which is that individual preferences are independent from the choices of other agents. Independent preferences are also assumed for the baseline version of the model of intertemporal choice. In the context of consumption analysis, social preferences mean that utility also depends on how one's own consumption compares to average consumption. In the case of 'catching up with the Joneses', agents' utility is usually assumed to depend on past average consumption. Agents' utility depends on *current* average consumption in the case of 'keeping up with the Joneses' assumption (e.g. Harbaugh, 1996; Clark & Oswald, 1998; Ljungqvist & Uhlig, 2000).

In both 'catching up with the Joneses' and 'keeping up with the Joneses' assumptions, consumption and saving patterns are different compared to the standard models with independent preferences. In the first case, if peers' consumption is on a growing trend, then undersaving (or overborrowing) will occur, while in the opposite case the model gives rise to underconsumption. In the second case, a consumption externality arises since agents who increase their consumption do not take into account their effect on the aggregate desire by other agents to 'catch up'. Both

[5] Interdependent preferences have a long presence in economics discourse, and they have been employed in a number of areas of economics. For the basic paper, see Pollak (1976), and for reviews, Drakopoulos (2011, 2012).

formulations imply strong multiplier effects and point to the traditional Keynesian demand-management policies (Ljungqvist & Uhlig, 2000; Ulph, 2014; De Giorgi et al., 2020).

One can argue that the above modifications to the standard RANK models also indicate an attempt to introduce social influences on consumption decisions. However, as Daria Pignalosa observes: "In this respect, one cannot fail to notice that the functional forms adopted in the Euler equation literature in order to capture social influences on consumption are far too rigid to accommodate all these entailments at the same time" (Pignalosa, 2025, p. 555). Furthermore, in most of these formulations, agent heterogeneity does not really involve social interactions among agents given that they do not admit the influence of the social environment on individual behaviour. Agent heterogeneity manifests itself in idiosyncratic shocks or fractions of households facing borrowing constraints.

Concluding Comments

This chapter started with the introduction and the establishment of the random walk theory of consumption with utility maximisers, forward-looking agents characterised by rational expectations (or Euler consumption equation). The clear message of this theory was the undermining of fiscal and monetary policy effects for economic stabilisation. The constrained utility maximiser model of individual behaviour became the theoretical basis of orthodox macroeconomics. The rise of the representative agent models (RANK) was almost parallel to the gradual emergence of the new neoclassical synthesis also known as DSGE theory. In spite of their theoretical dominance, there were serious problems regarding the empirical testing of the theory.

The empirical shortcomings of the basic model and the criticism—especially after the financial crisis of 2008—gave rise to the search for various functional forms adopted in the Euler equation, such as the TANK and HANK models, and agents with habitual and non-standard behaviour. The important observation regarding the introduction of agent heterogeneity, habits, and social preferences in the orthodox framework is that in most settings their policy implications resemble the "old" Keynesian ones: they indicate significant fiscal and monetary policy effects contrary to the standard policy conclusions of the typical RANK-based macroeconomic models. Our attention in the next chapter shifts to a discussion of "old Keynesian", post Keynesian, and other alternative approaches to consumption function.

References

Aoki, M. (2001). *Modeling Aggregate Behavior and Fluctuations in Economics: Stochastic Views of Interacting Agents.* Cambridge University Press.

Arrondel, L., Roger, M., & Savignac, F. (2014). *Wealth and Income in the Euro Area: Heterogeneity in Households' Behaviours?*, ECB Working Paper No 1709.

Attanasio, O., & Weber, G. (2010). Consumption and Saving: Models of Intertemporal Allocation and Their Implications for Public Policy. *Journal of Economic Literature, 48*(3), 693–751.

Attanasio, O., Kovacs, A., & Moran, P. (2020). *Temptation and Commitment: Understanding Hand-to-Mouth Behavior.* NBER Working Papers, 27944.

Auclert, A., Rognlie, M., & Straub, L. (2024). The Intertemporal Keynesian Cross. *Journal of Political Economy, 132*(12), 4068–4121.

Axtell, R., & Farmer, J. (2025). Agent-Based Modeling in Economics and Finance: Past, Present, and Future. *Journal of Economic Literature, 63*(1), 197–287.

Bernasconi, M., Levaggi, R., & Menoncin, F. (2020). Dynamic Tax Evasion with Habit Formation in Consumption. *The Scandinavian Journal of Economics, 122*(3), 966–992.

Bernheim, B. (1987). Dissaving after Retirement: Testing the Pure Life Cycle Hypothesis. In Z. Bodie, J. B. Shoven, & D. A. Wise (Eds.), *Issues in Pension Economics* (pp. 237–280). University of Chicago Press.

Bernheim, B., Skinner, J., & Weinberg, S. (2001). What Accounts for the Variation in Retirement Wealth among U.S. Households? *American Economic Review, 91*(4), 832–857.

Bilbiie, F. (2008). Limited Asset Market Participation, Monetary Policy and (Inverted) Aggregate Demand Logic. *Journal of Economic Theory, 140*(1), 162–196.

Bilbiie, F. (2020). The New Keynesian Cross. *Journal of Monetary Economics, 114*, 90–108.

Blanchard, O. (2016). Do DSGE Models Have a Future? *Policy Brief* 16–11: 1–4. Washington: Peterson Institute for International Economics.

Blanchard, O. (2025). *Convergence? Thoughts About the Evolution of Mainstream Macroeconomics over the Last 40 Years.* Peterson Institute for International Economics, Working Paper Series, No WP25-8: 1-30.

Bruni, L., & Sugden, R. (2007). The Road Not Taken: How Psychology was Removed from Economics, and How It Might Be Brought Back. *The Economic Journal, 117*, 146–173.

Campbell, J., & Mankiw, G. (1989). Consumption, Income, and Interest Rates: Reinterpreting The Time Series Evidence. *NBER Macroeconomics Annual, 4*, 185–216.

Campbell, J., & Mankiw, G. (1990). Permanent Income, Current Income, and Consumption. *Journal of Business and Economic Statistics, 8*(3), 265–279.

Campbell, J. Y., & Mankiw, G. (1991). The Response of Consumption to Income: A Cross-Country Investigation. *European Economic Review, 35*(4), 723–767.

Cantore, C., & Freund, L. (2021). Workers, Capitalists and the Government: Fiscal Policy and Income (Re)Distribution. *Journal of Monetary Economics, 119*, 58–74.

Carroll, C. (2001). A Theory of the Consumption Function, with and without Liquidity Constraints. *Journal of Economic Perspectives, 15*(3), 23–45.

Carroll, C., & Summers, L. (1991). Consumption Growth Parallels Income Growth: Some New Evidence. In B. D. Bernheim & J. B. Shoven (Eds.), *National Saving and Economic Performance* (pp. 305–348). University of Chicago Press.

Carroll, C., Crawley, E., Slacalek, J., Tokuoka, K., & White, M. (2020). Sticky Expectations and Consumption Dynamics. *American Economic Journal: Macroeconomics, 12*(3), 40–76.

Ciccarelli, M., Pariès, M. D., & Priftis, R. (2024). *ECB Macroeconometric Models for Forecasting and Policy Analysis.* ECB Occasional Paper Series, No. 344, pp. 1–110.

Clark, A., & Oswald, A. (1998). Comparison-Concave Utility and Following Behaviour in Social And Economic Settings. *Journal of Public Economics, 70*, 133–155.

De Giorgi, G., Frederiksen, A., & Pistaferri, L. (2020). Consumption Network Effects. *Review of Economic Studies, 87*(1), 130–163.

Deaton, A. (1992). *Macroeconomics and Consumption.* Oxford University Press.

Debortoli, D., & Galí, J. (2024). *Heterogeneity and Aggregate Fluctuations: Insights from TANK Models.* Barcelona School of Economics Working Papers No 1436: 1–43.

Drakopoulos, S. (2011). The Neglect of Comparison Income: An Historical Perspective. *European Journal of the History of Economic Thought, 18*(3), 441–464.

Drakopoulos, S. (2012). The History of Attitudes Towards Interdependent Preferences. *Journal of the History of Economic Thought, 34*(4), 541–557.

Drakopoulos, S., & Katselidis, I. (2019). Classical and Pre-Marginalist Ideas on the Relationship between Economics and Psychology. *History of Economic Ideas, 28*(1), 43–63.

Flavin, M. (1981). The Adjustment of Consumption to Changing Expectations about Future Income. *Journal of Political Economy, 89*(5), 974–1009.

Foster, J. (2021). The US Consumption Function: A New Perspective. *Journal of Evolutionary Economics, 31*, 773–798.

Fuhrer, J. (2000). Habit Formation in Consumption and Its Implications for Monetary-Policy Models. *American Economic Review, 90*(3), 367–390.

Galbacs, P. (2015). *The Theory of New Classical Macroeconomics: A Positive Critique*. Springer.

Galí, J., López-Salido, D., & Vallés, J. (2007). Understanding the Effects of Government Spending on Consumption. *Journal of the European Economic Association, 5*(1), 227–270.

García, C., Otero, D., & Salazar, B. (2023). The Drifting Influence of Hall's Random-Walk Hypothesis on Consumption Modeling. *History of Political Economy, 55*(1), 103–143.

Goodfriend, M., & King, R. (1997). The new Neoclassical Synthesis and the Role of Monetary Policy. In B. Bernanke & J. Rotemberg (Eds.), *NBER Macroeconomics Annual 1997* (pp. 231–296). MIT Press.

Goodwin, C. (2016). Economics and Psychology: Why the Great Divide? *History of Political Economy, 48*(Suppl. 1), 71–169.

Hall, R. E. (1978). Stochastic Implications of the Life Cycle-Permanent Income Hypothesis: Theory and Evidence. *Journal of Political Economy, 86*(6), 971–987.

Hamermesh, D. (1984). Consumption During Retirement: The Missing Link in the Life Cycle. *Review of Economics and Statistics, 66*(1), 1–7.

Hands, W. (2017). Conundrums of the Representative Agent. *Cambridge Journal of Economics, 41*, 1685–1704.

Harbaugh, R. (1996). Falling Beyond the Joneses: Relative Consumption and the Growth-Savings Paradox. *Economics Letters, 53*, 297–304.

Hartley, J. (1997). *The Representative Agent in Macroeconomics*. Routledge.

Hendry, D., & Muellbauer, J. (2018). The Future of Macroeconomics: Macro Theory and Models at the Bank of England. *Oxford Review of Economic Policy, 34*(1–2), 287–328.

Hoover, K. D. (2012). Microfoundational Programs. In P. G. Duarte & G. T. Lima (Eds.), *Microfoundations Reconsidered: The Relationship of Micro and Macroeconomics in Historical Perspective* (pp. 19–61). Edward Elgar.

Jappelli, T., & Pistaferri, L. (2017). *The Economics of Consumption: Theory and Evidence*. Oxford University Press.

Kaplan, G., Moll, B., & Violante, G. (2018). Monetary Policy According to HANK. *American Economic Review, 108*(3), 697–743.

Kiley, M. (2010). Habit Persistence, Nonseparability Between Consumption and Leisure, or Rule-of-Thumb Consumers: Which Accounts for the Predictability of Consumption Growth? *Review of Economics and Statistics, 92*(3), 679–683.

King, J. (2012). *The Microfoundations Delusion: Metaphor and Dogma in the History of Macroeconomics*. Edward Elgar.

Kirman, A. (1992). Whom or What Does the Representative Individual Represent? *Journal of Economic Perspectives, 6*, 117–136.

Laidler, D. (2010). Lucas, Keynes, and the Crisis. *Journal of the History of Economic Thought, 32*(1), 39–62.

Ljungqvist, L., & Uhlig, H. (2000). Tax Policy and Aggregate Demand Management Under Catching up with the Joneses. *American Economic Review, 90*(3), 356–366.

Lucas, R. E. (1972). Expectations and the Neutrality of Money. *Journal of Economic Theory, 4*(2), 103–124.

Marchionatti, R., & Sella, L. (2017). Is Neo-Walrasian Macroeconom(etr)ics a Dead End? An Assessment of Recent Criticisms of DSGE Models. *Journal of Post Keynesian Economics, 40*(4), 441–469.

Meeusen, W. (2011). Whither the Microeconomic Foundations of Macroeconomic Theory? *Brussels Economic Review, 54*(1), 51–80.

Muellbauer, J. (2016). *Macroeconomics and Consumption.* Economics Series Working Papers Paper, No. 811, University of Oxford, Department of Economics, Oxford, UK.

Muth, J. (1961). Rational Expectations and the Theory of Price Movements. *Econometrica, 29*(3), 315–335.

Pignalosa, D. (2021). The Euler Equation Approach: Critical Implications of Recent Developments in the Theory of Intertemporal Choice. *Bulletin of Political Economy, 15*(1), 1–43.

Pignalosa, D. (2025). Consumption as a Social Phenomenon in the Modern Theory of Intertemporal Choice. *Review of Political Economy, 37*(2), 543–563.

Pollak, R. (1976). Interdependent Preferences. *American Economic Review, 66*, 745–763.

Rizvi, S. (1994). The Microfoundations Project in General Equilibrium Theory. *Cambridge Journal of Economics, 18*(4), 357–377.

Siegel, J., & Thaler, R. (1997). Anomalies: The Equity Premium Puzzle. *Journal of Economic Perspectives, 11*(1), 191–200.

Stiglitz, J. (2018). Where Modern Macroeconomics Went Wrong. *Oxford Review of Economic Policy, 34*(1–2), 70–106.

Taylor, L. (2004). *Reconstructing Macroeconomics: Structuralist Proposals and Critiques of the Mainstream.* Harvard University Press.

Ulph, D. (2014). Keeping Up with the Joneses: Who Loses Out? *Economics Letters, 125*, 400–403.

Winter, J., Schlafmann, K., & Rodepeter, R. (2012). Rules of Thumb in Lifecycle Saving Decisions. *Economic Journal, 122*(560), 479–501.

Woodford, M. (2009). Convergence in Macroeconomics: Elements of the New Synthesis. *American Economic Journal: Macroeconomics, 1*(1), 267–279.

Zeldes, S. (1989). Consumption and Liquidity Constraints: An Empirical Investigation. *Journal of Political Economy, 97*(2), 305–346.

CHAPTER 8

Non-mainstream Approaches to Consumption

Introduction

Among other issues, the previous chapter discussed how the representative agent models became dominant in the new neoclassical synthesis also known as DSGE theory. It was maintained that the empirical failures of the theory led to modifications of the various functional forms adopted in the Euler equation, such as the TANK and HANK models, and agents with habitual and non-standard behaviour. Parallel to these developments, there were alternative approaches to aggregate consumption originating from non-mainstream authors and schools of thought. One common characteristic of these approaches was the rejection of utility maximising agents as a basis of consumption patterns. In particular, Michal Kalecki's approach was grounded on an entirely different framework involving socioeconomic classes instead of maximising individuals. The same holds for most members of the Cambridge, UK school such as Nicholas Kaldor and Luigi Pasinetti. Formulations pertaining to consumption have also emerged from the Post Keynesian school drawing in many respects from Keynes and the Kalecki-Kaldor-Pasinetti line of thought.

However, the heterodox economists were not the only ones criticising the basic assumptions and the underlying methodological framework of mainstream consumption functions. For example, Robert Clower and James Tobin attempted to develop further the original Keynesian approach (sometimes labelled as 'Old Keynesian') to aggregate consumption. This

S. A. Drakopoulos, *The Consumption Function in Economics*, https://doi.org/10.1007/978-3-032-15958-8_8

chapter will start with a discussion of their views, focusing mainly on the work of James Tobin. It will proceed with a presentation of Kalecki and Kaleckian-based approaches, and with the theories developed by Kaldor and Pasinetti. Finally, it will outline the broad common elements concerning aggregate consumption found in the contemporary Post Keynesian school.

Keynesian Approaches to Consumption: James Tobin

Concerning the analysis of aggregate consumption patterns and the establishment of the Neoclassical approach to macroeconomics presented in the previous chapter (Chap. 7), there was a reaction coming from 'old' or 'traditional' Keynesian framework. A primary example was the 'dual-decision hypothesis' suggested by Robert Clower. In particular, Clower's (1965) work challenged the standard Neoclassical assumption that consumers always optimise based on their full income potential. He argued that when involuntary unemployment exists, households adjust their consumption and savings decisions based on their constrained income, rather than on equilibrium wage. This perspective linked demand shortfalls in the goods market to persistent unemployment, offering a more dynamic explanation of Keynesian unemployment beyond simple wage stickiness. In the same vein, Axel Leijonhufvud (1967) built on Clower's insights by arguing that Keynes' original vision, particularly in *The General Theory*, was not just about wage rigidity, but about broader coordination failures in the economy.[1] On the issue of adhering to Keynes' approach to consumption, the work of James Meade also deserves to be mentioned. In his *An Introduction to Economic Analysis and Policy,* Meade does not invoke utility maximisation or any other aspect of the neoclassical theory of consumer behaviour (Meade, 1936, pp. 49–60).

James Tobin's work can be viewed as a characteristic case of Post-WWII Keynesian-oriented theorists (e.g. Eichengreen, 2020). Tobin called himself an "Old Keynesian" in contrast to New Keynesian, New Classical, and Post Keynesian economics (Dimand, 2010). As an indication of his Keynesian-based analytical framework, Tobin supported the need for fiscal and monetary policy, arguing that the normal operation of an 'unaided'

[1] Don Patinkin, Robert Clower, and Axel Leijonhufvud among others challenged the neoclassical synthesis and argued that the notion of disequilibrium formed a fundamental part of Keynes' theory (see also Tsoulfidis, 2024).

modern market economy is likely to lead to inefficient, socially costly outcomes. In particular, he believed that there was a distinct role for fiscal policy in stabilisation policy (for a discussion, see Buiter, 2003, pp. 601–615). Further, his attack on Monetarism, one of the dominant macroeconomic schools of his age with strong anti-Keynesian policy recommendations, was also indicative (Tobin, 1981).

Along with other major theoretical contributions to macroeconomics, household consumption and saving patterns were an important part of Tobin's research and policy agenda from the beginning of his academic career (for an extensive summary of his contributions, see Buiter, 2003; Dimand, 2014; see also Myhrman, 1982).[2] In his early work, Tobin (1951) tested the relative income hypothesis against the absolute income hypothesis. In line with several works of that period, he found differences between the cross-sectional and short-run evidence (indicating that the average propensity to consume declining with the level of income), with the long-run evidence (indicating a constant APC). He also observed that the cross-section consumption functions for whites were higher than those for blacks, and the average sample income was higher for whites. This finding was supportive of the relative income hypothesis. However, he stressed that the evidence was consistent with the hypothesis that black families have lower levels of financial wealth than whites and are therefore in a poorer position to smooth consumption in the face of transitory shocks (Tobin, 1951).

It has been argued that Tobin's argumentation was an early exposition of the role of liquidity constraints in the consumption function (Hynes, 1998). Further, Tobin employed the hypothesis that rising financial wealth could reconcile the cross-sectional and short-run evidence with the long-run evidence. As was seen in Chap. 6, this was the core of the life-cycle model by Modigliani and Brumberg. The consideration of wealth as playing a part in the consumption decisions is linked to Tobin's influence by Irving Fisher's approach to intertemporal choice (Fisher, 1930; see also Buiter, 2003). Tobin developed further his analysis of consumption and savings patterns by elaborating the notion of liquidity constraints that became central in his subsequent works (with Walt Dolde). Liquidity constraints characterise the optimal consumption plan of many households, especially those with 'permanent income preferences' and a rising age-earnings profile. These works introduced a version of realistic permanent income/life-cycle models with

[2] Tobin's (1947) doctoral dissertation was on consumption and saving, introducing wealth as well as income as an argument in the consumption function.

liquidity constraints that bind at certain points in the life cycle (Tobin & Dolde, 1971; Dolde & Tobin, 1983; see also Buiter, 2003).

In spite of his 'partial' acceptance of the life-cycle model, Tobin had expressed serious reservations regarding the representative agent assumption, popularised in macroeconomics since the 1970s by the New Classical school. He had a deep mistrust of the notion and viewed it as a crucial oversimplification (Tobin, 1983; see also Buiter, 2003, p. 588). Tobin held that representative agent models were totally unsuited for analysing the macroeconomic coordination problem posed by Keynes (for discussions, see Dimand, 2004, 2010). In general, he thought that the representative agent model was on the top of his list of unfortunate developments in macroeconomic theory during his lifetime (Buiter, 2003, p. 618).

Tobin held that macroeconomic models should be consistent with the knowledge of the behaviour of individual economic units and particular markets. However, he was pessimistic about this issue emphasising the problem of aggregation over individuals and assets (see also Myhrman, 1982). As he wrote: "Unfortunately it is seldom true that an exact relationship among aggregate variables, independent of their composition, can be built up from the basis of microeconomic relationships" (Tobin, 1971, p. ix). Moreover, it is important to point out that he referred to "the behavior of individual economic units" and not to the optimising behaviour. In his opinion, microfoundations are not synonymous with constrained optimisation, believing that constrained optimisation was not "the only permissible way to generate decision rules or other characterisations of individual behaviour, like Euler equations" (Buiter, 2003, p. 615). In fact, Tobin was interested in the broader behavioural and psychological approaches to economic behaviour (Tobin & Dolbear, 1963). This stance was also indicative of his non-dogmatic approach to economic methodology (see also Buiter, 2003, pp. 616–618). Tobin's methodological position was another aspect (among the many), which clearly differentiated him from the orthodox macroeconomic schools of his era.

Michal Kalecki and Kaleckian-Based Approaches to Consumption

Michal Kalecki is considered to be a major figure in the development of contemporary heterodox macroeconomic thought. Many eminent Post Keynesian figures have expressed their great appreciation of his contributions and acknowledge him as one of the pillars of Post Keynesian school of thought (see for instance, Joan Robinson, 1980, and Geoff Harcourt, 1977). Contemporary Post Keynesians also point out Kalecki's profound impact on the theoretical development of heterodox and Post Keynesian economics (e.g. Sawyer, 1985; Arestis, 1996; for a review of Kalecki's influence, see Rochon et al., 2020).

Classical political economy, and especially the Ricardian-Marx tradition, had a major impact on Kalecki's economic thinking (Brennan, 2022). The central role of the notion of two socioeconomic classes (workers and capitalists), and his emphasis on the problems of economic growth and income distribution indicated his strong classical political economy influences.[3] Further, Kalecki made virtually no use of standard concepts and tools of neoclassical economics such as the utility function, the production function, and equilibrium (Kalecki, 1971; see also Sawyer, 1985, pp. 9–14).

Similar to Keynes, aggregate consumption and savings patterns also play an important role in his economic analysis. According to Kalecki and following King's (2013) and Hein's (2017) presentations, let us assume a simple framework of a closed economy with no state sector. In this setting, total expenditure is comprised by aggregate consumption (C) and aggregate investment (I). Consumption is divided into consumption spending by workers and capitalists.

$$C = Cw + Cp \tag{8.1}$$

In Eq. 8.1, Cw refers to consumption spending by workers, and Cp to consumption spending by capitalists. In Kalecki's analysis, there is no saving by workers but only by capitalists, meaning that:

$$Cw = W \tag{8.2}$$

Total income (Y) equals total wages plus total profits (P):

$$Y = W + P \tag{8.3}$$

[3] The marginal revolution in economics involved a shift in focus, from society and social class to the individual, and a corresponding shift in problem area, from production and distribution to consumption and exchange (see also Dobb, 1973).

Given (Eq. 8.1), (Eq. 8.2), and (Eq. 8.3), and the equality of expenditure and income, total profits are:

$$P = Cp + I \tag{8.4}$$

Thus and as Eq. 8.4 indicates, aggregate, profits are determined by capitalists' expenditure (King, 2013, pp. 487–488).[4]

In a more detailed analytical setting, the consumption of capitalists can be written as:

$$Cp = A + cpP \tag{8.5}$$

In Eq. 8.5, A is constant consumption and cp is the propensity to consume or the propensity to save out of profits (sp = 1- cp). Combining Eqs. (8.4) and (8.5) and given that sp = 1-cp, total profits are:

$$P = \frac{A + I}{1 - cp} = \frac{A + I}{sp} \tag{8.6}$$

Equation 8.6 shows that profits are determined by capitalists' (fairly constant) consumption, investment expenditure (variable/cyclical), and by the propensity to consume or the propensity to save out of profits (Nuti, 2004, p. 98).

In a more general framework, Kalecki argued that most markets in capitalism are characterised by a degree of monopoly, and therefore the profit share depends on the degree of monopoly in product markets (and also, in his later work, on the outcome of class conflict in the labour market). Furthermore, fluctuations in investment expenditure are the key to the business cycle, but similar to Keynes, there is also a tendency for a chronic deficiency in effective demand (King, 2013, p. 488).

It must be noted that the analysis of consumption patterns in Kalecki's work is rather limited. The main reason is that "capitalism is not to be analysed in terms of consumption as the final aim (whereas neoclassical economics is founded on such an analysis), but rather that profits are the central driving force of the system" (Sawyer, 1985, p. 72).

[4] In an open economy model with state sector, aggregate profits depend on expenditure by capitalists plus the budget deficit plus the trade surplus (King, 2013).

The influence of the works of Kalecki, Kaldor, and Pasinetti on subsequent heterodox approaches to consumption is easily discernable. Following this tradition, the focus of most works is on the issues of income distribution, business cycles, and economic growth. Consumption patterns analysis is rather indirect and mostly related to its role in the above-mentioned themes (for a review of the main arguments, see Hein, 2023 and references therein). We will very briefly outline a couple of indicative examples. In a recent paper, Carlo D'Ippoliti and Francesco Linguanti (2023) develop a short-run neo-Kaleckian model to investigate the interplay of the functional and personal distribution of income and their impact on growth. The authors utilise the institutionalist hypothesis of consumption emulation which makes aggregate saving dependent on the concentration of wages and profits. The analysis of savings is conducted in terms of the Kaleckian two socioeconomic classes. In their framework, consumption emulation implies that personal income inequality increases the marginal propensity to save and therefore it reduces aggregate consumption. In accordance with Keynes' basic insight, a more equal distribution of wages and/or profits increases aggregate demand and the rate of capacity utilisation (D'Ippoliti & Linguanti, 2023).

Other papers specify an explicit consumption function in their macroeconomic models. For instance, Onaran et al. (2011) write the consumption function as follows:

$$C = c0 + cwY + cp\left(cp - cw\right)\pi Y \tag{8.7}$$

In Eq. 8.7, C is total consumption, c0 is autonomous consumption, Y is income, cp and cw are the marginal propensity to consume out of profits and out of wages, respectively, and π is the profit share. The relevance of income distribution in a consumption function is that cw—the propensity to consume out of wages—is higher than that out of profits written as cp:

$$\left(cp - cw\right) < 0 \tag{8.8}$$

Thus, Eq. (8.7) indicates that consumption is expected to decrease when the profit share in income (π) rises. In general, the subsequent Kaleckian-based consumption formulations contain the core elements of Michael Kalecki analysis: consumption behaviour differs among income categories; workers receive wages and capitalists receive profits, including retained earnings, dividends, interest, and rent; the propensity to consume out of wages is higher than that out of profits. Finally, the notion of class-based consumption patterns as well as other key notions such as the political business cycle, indicate the political and sociological dimensions in Kalecki's analysis (see also Olters, 2004).

Consumption in the Works of Nicholas Kaldor and Luigi Pasinetti

Kalecki's insights influenced the Cambridge (UK) Post Keynesians, especially Joan Robinson, Nicholas Kaldor, Richard Goodwin, and Luigi Pasinetti, as well as modern American Post Keynesian economists. Although a detailed analysis of aggregate consumption was not a main theme in their works, we will present the views on consumption of Kaldor and Pasinetti. Kaldor's ideas on aggregate consumption can be found indirectly in his analysis of income distribution, and also in his works on economic growth (i.e. Kaldor, 1955–1956; 1957). Contrary to the Neoclassical approach, Kaldor (1955–1956) adopts the classical notion of socioeconomic classes (workers and capitalists), also contained in Kalecki's analysis. His main aim was to describe "a model which shows the distribution of income to be determined by the Keynesian investment-savings mechanism" (Kaldor, 1955–1956, p. 97). In the process of building his theory of distribution, Kaldor assumes full employment and therefore a given total output or income (Y) that can be divided between consumption C) and investment (I). In Kaldor's system, the equation of total consumption is:

$$C = cwW + cpP \tag{8.9}$$

In Eq. 8.9, W is wages, P is profits, and cw and cp are the propensities to consume out of wages and out of profits, respectively. In his words "...the wage-category comprises not only manual labour but salaries as well, and Profits the income of property owners generally, and not only of entrepreneur..." (Kaldor, 1955–1956, p. 95). The corresponding propensities to save out of wages and out of profits are *sw* and *sp* (both being no less than zero and no more than unity), and total savings are:

$$S = swW + spP \tag{8.10}$$

According to Kaldor, the model operates only if the two savings propensities differ and the propensity to save from profits exceeds that from wages:

$$sp \neq sw \text{ and } sp > sw \qquad (8.11)$$

It has to be noted that Kaldor wanted to suggest an alternative distribution theory without the neoclassical assumptions and tools. He also acknowledged the link of his approach to other related theories. In his words:

> *We have seen how the various 'models' of distribution, the Ricardo-Marxian, the Keynesian and the Kaleckian are related to each other. I am not sure where 'marginal productivity' comes in in all this.* (Kaldor, 1955–1956, p. 100)

During the same period, Franco Modigliani reacted to Kaldor's formulations in terms of consumption patterns based on the notion of two different social classes. In a joint paper with Paul Samuelson, they denied any meaning of the capitalists' marginal propensity to save (Samuelson & Modigliani, 1966, p. 329). The same tone is present in another joint paper (almost a decade later) that aimed "to provide overwhelming evidence against the standard Kaldorian two cast parable of hard-pressed workers … and plush capitalists," and to overcome the classical class division in a model where "every household is typically both a worker and a recipient of property income during at least some phase of the LC [Life Cycle]" (Modigliani & Tarantelli, 1975, p. 825). The debate concerning the consumption and savings functions also revealed the fundamental differences between the Neoclassical and the Post Keynesian conceptual frameworks (for a detailed discussion, see Rancan, 2019).

Luigi Pasinetti also contributed to the theory of distribution originating from the Cambridge school. Similar to Kaldor, Pasinetti was interested in the interaction between income distribution, economic growth, and the pattern of consumption (i.e. Pasinetti, 1974). In his work on the extension of Kaldor's theory of distribution, Pasinetti rejected the criticism of the classification of the members of a modern society in only two groups (Pasinetti, 1962, p. 279). In his own version of the theory of distribution, Pasinetti adopted Kaldor's model but assumed that workers also saved and owned part of the stock of capital, from which they earned some profits. This meant that total profits are the sum of profits accrued to capitalists

(Pp) and profits which accrue to the workers (Pw) (Pasinetti, 1962, p. 270). The total savings function now becomes (following Kaldor's notation):

$$S = sw\left(W + Pw\right) + spPp \tag{8.12}$$

Pasinetti showed that the rate of profit in the Kaldorian growth equilibrium was independent of the labourers' saving propensities, depending only on the savings rate of capitalists.[5] His argument generated controversy among orthodox theorists of that time. Like in the case of Kaldor, Samuelson and Modigliani pointed to the unrealistic assumption of "artificial" subdivision of population into labourers and capitalists (Samuelson & Modigliani, 1966, p. 329; Rancan, 2019 supplies a detailed discussion).

Post Keynesian Approaches to Consumption

Although there are still ongoing debates regarding the basic core of the Post Keynesian school of thought, it seems that one can distinguish some common general ideas. Apart from Keynes, the school draws from a number of different research traditions (Arestis, 1996; Hein, 2023). A good example in this respect is the analysis of aggregate consumption patterns where ideas from Kalecki, Kaldor, and Pasinetti are combined with Keynes' notion of fundamental uncertainty and with an alternative conception of individual rationality.[6] The unbounded rationality or hyper-model-consistent rationality frequently used in most mainstream macroeconomic formulations is certainly rejected as unrealistic (Baddeley, 2017; Lavoie, 2022). The notion of Herbert Simon's 'bounded rationality' is viewed as more appropriate in an environment of uncertainty (Arestis, 1996; King, 2013).[7] Further, a number of Post Keynesian approaches to aggregate consumption employ the framework of hierarchical (lexicographic) choice

[5] Pasinetti arrived at the modified 'Cambridge equation' given as $I = swY + P(sp - sw)$. See also Panico and Salvadori (1993)).

[6] It has been argued that heterodox schools of economic thought (including Marxist, Kaleckians, Sraffians, and Post Keynesians) share some basic principles regarding economic rationality (e.g. Lavoie, 2006).

[7] Fundamental uncertainty should be seen in conjunction with Keynes' notion of 'animal spirits' referring to investment decisions by entrepreneurs (Laine, 2017; Lavoie, 2022).

as a baseline, instead of the mainstream utility maximising theory of choice (for discussions, see Lavoie, 1994; Drakopoulos, 1994, 1999; Aboobaker, 2024). Consequently, the vast majority of Post Keynesians reject the standard assumption of rational expectations underlying the DSGE models that were discussed previously (for the basic paper, see Davidson, 1982–1983). Further, the methodological framework of mainstream microfoundations of macroeconomic models employed by DSGE literature is also rejected (e.g. King, 2012).

The Post Keynesian approach emphasises Keynes' notion of fundamental uncertainty: "when the value of an outcome is unknown, when the probability of an outcome is unknown, when the outcomes that can possibly result from a choice are unknown, or when the spectrum of possible choices is unknown" (Lavoie, 2022, p. 76; also Davidson, 1991). This type of uncertainty, sometimes called Knightian or Keynesian uncertainty, is virtually ignored by mainstream analysis in which uncertainty is solely measured by statistical variance (see also Dow, 2023). It has been maintained that the concept of fundamental uncertainty is the basic distinguishing characteristic of the Post Keynesians as a school of economic thought. As Tony Lawson observes: "Post Keynesians, for example, make fundamental uncertainty a central category. This clearly presupposes an ontology of openness as many post Keynesians have in recent years come increasingly to acknowledge" (Lawson, 2009, p. 125).

Fundamental uncertainty leads households to put more savings in liquid assets in order to be able to dissolve these savings without costs in future periods.[8] The marginal propensity to consume decreases if uncertainty rises, which gives the equivalent to the precautionary saving motive (for a detailed discussion, see Menz, 2010). Further, the notion of fundamental uncertainty poses serious challenges to the orthodox consumption formulations like the permanent/life-cycle theories. It is indicative that Modigliani himself recognised it as an unresolved issue since the earliest days, admitting that the main effect of uncertainty would be to generate a demand for precautionary saving—a motive that had been recognised at least as early as Keynes (see Deaton, 2005). Just as Keynes (1937, p. 214) clearly implies, consumption decisions under fundamental uncertainty involve following social norms, rules of thumb, or experts' opinion. Attempting to integrate the social aspects of consumption, some Post Keynesian literature also refers to Duesenberry's relative consumption

[8] As was mentioned in Chap. 3, John Commons held a similar view (Tymoigne, 2003).

hypothesis, combining it with the idea that the saving rate is closely related to the position within the income distribution (e.g. Palley, 2010).

Another related and rather common characteristic of Post Keynesian consumption formulations is the classification of consumption spending by workers, and consumption spending by capitalists. Influenced by the Cambridge tradition, it is also supplemented by the fundamental assumption that the propensity to consume is lower for profits than for wages (e.g. Arestis, 1996; King, 2013). Finally and in terms of economic policy recommendations, fiscal policy (and to a lesser extent monetary policy) is considered a crucial tool for economic stabilisation (e.g. Arestis & Sawyer, 2003; for reviews, see also Hein, 2017; Blecker and Setterfield, 2019). Contrary to Neoclassical policy conclusions, "deficit-financed government expenditure was an important weapon against demand-deficient unemployment, while budget surpluses should be used to restrain demand-push inflation" (King, 2013, p. 496).

Concluding Comments

This chapter concentrated on the non-mainstream approaches to aggregate consumption patterns. After discussing Tobin's criticism of mainstream formulations based on his Keynesian influences, it proceeded to Kalecki's theory. Kalecki did not focus on consumption as such, but his views were part of his broad analysis of income distribution. In the same vein, Kaldor and Pasinetti employed consumption functions in their works investigating issues of income distribution and economic growth in capitalist economies. Contemporary Post Keynesians engage in criticism of the standard consumption formulations, also drawing from Keynes and other heterodox views.

One can discern some common points pertaining to aggregate consumption in the above analyses. The rejection of the concept of representative agent and the central assumption of optimising behaviour of agents are two prime examples. The belief of the need of economic policies for the stabilisation of capitalism is another important common point. Those common ideas found in seemingly different approaches such as in the writings of Kalecki and Tobin lead us to investigate the methodological foundations of different approaches to aggregate consumption in the next chapter.

References

Aboobaker, A. (2024). Hierarchical Consumption Preferences, Redistribution, and Structural Transformation. *Industrial and Corporate Change, 33*, 490–506.

Arestis, P. (1996). Post-Keynesian Economics: Towards Coherence. *Cambridge Journal of Economics, 20*(1), 111–135.

Arestis, P., & Sawyer, M. (2003). Reinventing Fiscal Policy. *Journal of Post Keynesian Economics, 26*(1), 3–26.

Baddeley, M. (2017). Keynes's Psychology and Behavioural Macroeconomics: Theory and Policy. *Economic and Labour Relations Review, 28*(2), 177–196.

Blecker, R., & Setterfield, M. (2019). *Heterodox Macroeconomics: Models of Demand, Distribution and Growth*. Edward Elgar Publishing.

Brennan, D. (2022). Beyond Profit-Led versus Investment-Led Capitalism: Marx and Kalecki on 'Capitalists' Consumption' and 'Workers' Savings. *Rethinking Marxism, 34*(3), 294–316.

Buiter, W. (2003). James Tobin: An Appreciation of His Contribution to Economics. *The Economic Journal, 113*(491), 585–631.

Clower, R. (1965). The Keynesian Counterrevolution: A Theoretical Appraisal. In F. H. Hahn & F. P. R. Brechling (Eds.), *The Theory of Interest Rates* (pp. 103–125). Macmillan.

D'Ippoliti, C., & Linguanti, F. (2023). Inequality, Consumption Emulation, and Growth. *Review of Radical Political Economics, 55*(4), 577–590.

Davidson, P. (1982–1983). Rational Expectations: A Fallacious Foundation for Studying Crucial Decision Making Processes. *Journal of Post Keynesian Economics, 5*(2), 182–198.

Davidson, P. (1991). Is Probability Theory Relevant for Uncertainty? A Post-Keynesian Perspective. *Journal of Economic Perspectives, 5*(1), 129–143.

Deaton, A. (2005). Franco Modigliani and the Life-Cycle Theory of Consumption. *BNL Quarterly Review, LVIII*(233–234), 91–107.

Dimand, R. (2004). James Tobin and the Transformation of the IS-LM Model in M. De Vroey and K. Hoover (Eds.), The IS-LM Model: Its Rise, Fall, and Strange Persistence, Duke University Press, Annual Supplement to *History of Political Economy* 36: 165–189.

Dimand, R. (2010). Tobin's Keynesianism. In B. Bateman, T. Hirai, & M. C. Marcuzzo (Eds.), *The Return to Keynes, proceedings of Tokyo symposium on Keynes* (pp. 94–107). Belknap Press of Harvard University Press.

Dimand, R. (2014). *James Tobin (Great Thinkers in Economics)*. Palgrave Macmillan.

Dobb, M. (1973). *Theories of Value and Distribution Since Adam Smith: Ideology and Economic Theory*. Cambridge University Press.

Dolde, W., & Tobin, J. (1983). Mandatory Retirement Saving and Capital Formation. In F. Modigliani & R. Hemming (Eds.), *The Determinants of National Saving and Wealth* (pp. 56–88). Macmillan Press.

Dow, S. (2023). Uncertainty and Macroeconomic Methodology. In J. Jespersen, V. Chick, & B. Tieben (Eds.), *Routledge Handbook of Macroeconomic Methodology* (pp. 85–108). Routledge.

Drakopoulos, S. (1994). Hierarchical Choice in Economics. *Journal of Economic Surveys, 8*(2), 133–153.

Drakopoulos, S. (1999). Post-Keynesian Choice Theory. In P. A. O'Hara (Ed.), *Encyclopedia of Political Economy Volume 2* (pp. 887–889). Routledge.

Eichengreen, B. (2020). Keynesian Economics: Can It Return if It Never Died? *Review of Keynesian Economics, 8*(1), 23–35.

Fisher, I. (1930). *The Theory of Interest.* Macmillan.

Harcourt, G. (1977). Review of The Intellectual Capital of Michal Kalecki. *Economica, 44*(173), 92–94.

Hein, E. (2017). The principle of effective demand: Marx, Kalecki, Keynes, and beyond. In T.-H. Jo, L. Chester, & C. D'Ippoliti (Eds.), *The Routledge Handbook of Heterodox Economics: Theorizing, Analyzing, and Transforming Capitalism* (pp. 84–100). Routledge.

Hein, E. (2017). Post-Keynesian Macroeconomics since the mid 1990s: Main Developments. *European Journal of Economics and Economic Policies,* 14(2), 131–172.

Hein, E. (2023). *Macroeconomics after Kalecki and Keynes: Post-Keynesian Foundations.* Edward Elgar.

Hynes, A. H. (1998). The Emergence of The Neoclassical Consumption Function: The Formative Years. 1940–1952. *Journal of the History of Economic Thought, 20*(01), 25–49.

Kaldor N. (1955–1956). Alternative Theories of Distribution. *The Review of Economics Studies, 23*(2): 83–100.

Kaldor, N. (1957). A Model of Economic Growth. *Economic Journal, 67*(268), 591–624.

Kalecki, M. (1971). *Selected Essays on the Dynamics of the Capitalist Economy.* Cambridge University Press.

Keynes, J. M. (1937). The General Theory of Employment. *Quarterly Journal of Economics, 51*(2), 209–223.

King, J. (2012). *The Microfoundations Delusion: Metaphor and Dogma in the History of Macroeconomics.* Edward Elgar.

King, J. (2013). An Introduction to Post Keynesian Macroeconomics. *Jahrgang, 39*(4), 485–507.

Laine, M. (2017). The Heterogeneity of Animal Spirits: A Taxonomy of Entrepreneurs with Regard to Investment Decisions. *Cambridge Journal of Economics, 41*(2), 595–636.

Lavoie, M. (1994). A Post Keynesian Theory of Consumer Choice. *Journal of Post Keynesian Economics, 16*(4), 539–562.

Lavoie, M. (2006). Do Heterodox Theories Have Anything in Common? A Post-Keynesian Point of View. *European Journal of Economics and Economic Policies: Intervention, 3*(1), 87–112.

Lavoie, M. (2022). *Post-Keynesian Economics: New Foundations* (2nd ed.). Edward Elgar.

Lawson, T. (2009). Heterodox Economics and Pluralism: reply to Davis. In E. Fullbrook (Ed.), *Ontology and Economics: Tony Lawson and His Critics* (pp. 93–129). Routledge.

Leijonhufvud, A. (1967). Keynes and the Keynesians: A Suggested Interpretation. *The American Economic Review, 57*(2), 401–410.

Meade, J. (1936). *An Introduction to Economic Analysis and Policy.* Oxford University Press.

Menz, J.-O. (2010). Uncertainty, Social Norms and Consumption Theory: Post and New Keynesian Approaches. *Intervention. European Journal of Economics and Economic Policies, 7*(1), 125–146.

Modigliani, F., & Tarantelli, E. (1975). The Consumption Function in a Developing Economy and the Italian Experience. *American Economic Review, 65*(5), 825–842.

Myhrman, J. (1982). James Tobin's Contributions to Economics. *The Scandinavian Journal of Economics, 84*(1), 89–99.

Nuti, D. (2004). Kalecki and Keynes Revisited: Two Original Approaches to Demand-Determined Income—And Much More Besides. In Z. Sadowski & A. Szeworski (Eds.), *Kalecki's Economics Today* (pp. 93–103). Routledge.

Olters, J.-P. (2004). The Political Business Cycle at Sixty: Towards a Neo-Kaleckian Understanding of Political Economy? *Cahiers d'économie Politique, 46*(1), 91–130.

Onaran, O., Stockhammer, E., & Grafl, L. (2011). Financialisation, Income Distribution and Aggregate Demand in the USA. *Cambridge Journal of Economics, 35*(4), 637–661.

Palley, T. (2010). Relative Permanent Income Theory of Consumption: A Synthetic Keynes-Duesenberry-Friedman Model. *Review of Political Economy, 22*(1), 41–56.

Panico, C., & Salvadori, N. (1993). *Post Keynesian Theory of Growth and Distribution.* Edward Elgar.

Pasinetti, L. (1962). Rate of Profit and Income Distribution in Relation to the Rate of Economic Growth. *The Review of Economic Studies, 29*(4), 267–279.

Pasinetti, L. (1974). *Growth and Income Distribution.* Cambridge University Press.

Rancan, A. (2019). Income Distribution, Consumption, and Economic Growth in Italy: Kaldor's Theory versus the Life Cycle Hypothesis, 1960s and 1970s. *History of Political Economy, 51*(5), 867–900.

Robinson, J. (1980). *Further Contributions to Modern Economics*. Blackwell.

Rochon, L.-P., Czachor, M., & Bachurewicz, G. (2020). Introduction: Kalecki and Kaleckian Economics. *Review of Political Economy, 32*(4), 487–491.

Samuelson, P., & Modigliani, F. (1966). The Pasinetti Paradox in Neoclassical and More General Models. *The Review of Economic Studies, 33*(4), 269–301.

Sawyer, M. (1985). *The Economics of Michał Kalecki*. Springer.

Tobin, J. (1947). *A Theoretical and Statistical Analysis of Consumer Saving*. Harvard University Ph.D. Thesis.

Tobin, J. (1951). Relative Income, Absolute Income, and Saving. Reprinted in *Essays in Economics, 2: Consumption and Econometrics*. MIT Press, 1987.

Tobin, J. (1971). *Essays in Economics, Volume 1, Macroeconomics*. Markham Publishing Company.

Tobin, J. (1981). The Monetarist Counter-Revolution Today—An Appraisal. *The Economic Journal, 91*(361), 29–42.

Tobin, J. (1983). Liquidity Preference, Separation and Asset Pricing. *Zeitschrift fiir Betriebswirtschaft, 3*, 53–57.

Tobin, J., & Dolbear, F. (1963). On the Relevance of Psychology to Economic Theory and Research. In S. Koch (Ed.), *Psychology: A Study of Science* (Vol. 6, pp. 677–684). McGraw-Hill.

Tobin, J., & Dolde, W. (1971). Wealth, Liquidity, Consumption. In *Consumer Spending and Monetary Policy: The Linkages*, Federal Reserve Bank of Boston, Conference Series No. 5.

Tsoulfidis, L. (2024). *Competing Schools of Economic Thought*. Springer.

Tymoigne, E. (2003). Keynes and Commons on Money. *Journal of Economic Issues, 37*(3), 527–545.

CHAPTER 9

The Methodological Framework of Aggregate Consumption Analysis

Introduction

Chapter 7 discussed the place of aggregate consumption in contemporary orthodox macroeconomic theory, and especially in the now dominant DSGE models. It was observed that consumption in this framework is part of a wider theoretical and methodological framework which is characterised by some fundamental components. The need for microeconomic foundations, expressed in the form of the representative agent that is based on the standard theory of expected utility maximising consumer, is one of those fundamental components of orthodoxy. Methodological individualism with its core feature that all economic interactions—including aggregate consumption—are to be explained in terms of individual behaviour is the other basic organising characteristic. Chapter 8 presented the heterodox alternative including the treatment of consumption by major Post Keynesian economists. The discussion indicated that aggregate consumption in Post Keynesian approaches is analysed in a different conceptual framework which is quite distant from notions such as the representative agent.

This chapter will focus on the underlying methodology of the above two different currents of macroeconomic thought. Its main aim is to present the conceptual setting in which aggregate consumption is integrated. It will also discuss the major criticisms that have been applied to this setting by various economists belonging to different intellectual traditions,

S. A. Drakopoulos, *The Consumption Function in Economics*,
https://doi.org/10.1007/978-3-032-15958-8_9

including heterodox macroeconomists. The chapter will commence with a brief overview of the main strands of contemporary mainstream macroeconomics. It will then consider its three fundamental components which are microfoundations, the role of the representative agent, and the unifying framework of methodological individualism. The chapter will continue with a brief overview of the heterodox macroeconomics related to the above issues.

Contemporary Strands of Mainstream Macroeconomics

There are three dominant strands of contemporary mainstream or orthodox macroeconomics which are the New Classical DSGE, the New Keynesian DSGE, and the real business cycle models (RBC). All of the above share a number of crucial assumptions such as (a) optimising behaviour of consumers and firms, (b) the rational expectations hypothesis, (c) an environment of complete markets, and (d) zero transactions costs. In addition, they all favour general equilibrium models and have as their benchmark the model of the representative agent (see, for instance: Carroll, 2000, 2001; Duarte, 2012; King, 2012; Muellbauer, 2016; Stiglitz, 2018). In regard to the assumption of complete markets, the distinguishing feature of New Keynesian DSGE models is that they include a number of market distortions such as nominal rigidities and monopolistic competition (King, 2012; Muellbauer, 2016).

The conception of future uncertainty is usually in known probabilities terms in an environment of risk, and effectively it does not play an important role in consumers' decisions (Lavoie, 2022). For instance, uncertainty in 'perfect foresight' formulations is simply assumed away (Carroll, 2001, pp. 25–26). Some versions employ the notion of certainty equivalence (or approximate certainty equivalence). Generally, certainty equivalence assumes that behaviour in an environment of uncertain income and health, and so forth, "can be closely approximated by behaviour for which uncertainty does not much matter" (Muellbauer, 2016, p. 5). In the specific context of macroeconomics, Ricardian equivalence is the idea that an increase in the budget deficit bequeaths a debt that has to be serviced with higher taxes in the future. Under restrictive conditions, the present value of the additional taxes will exactly equal the present value of the additional government spending (Eichengreen, 2020, p. 26). As Carroll has shown, the perfect foresight and certainty equivalent solutions are very similar (Carroll, 2001).[1]

Microfoundations

Keynes' theory and especially his consumption function did not have any foundations on the theory of individual choice (Blaug, 1968, p. 302). Keynes consciously rejected the need for microufoundations on methodological grounds, given his serious reservations regarding the expected utility maximising model, and the fallacy of composition (Jespersen, 2009; Chick & Jespersen, 2023; see also Chap. 3). Further, his repeated assertion of the need to provide a "theory of Output and Employment *as a whole*" reinforces the previous points (Keynes, 1936, p. 293, emphasis on the original). Similar to Keynes in this respect, Friedman had strong views against moving from the individual consumption function to aggregate consumption (Friedman, 1957).[2] In his opinion, the functional form of the aggregate consumption function will not be the same as that for the individual consumption function, and he makes no attempt to derive the functional form of the aggregate consumption function. Due to individual heterogeneities (age, income and wealth variations, family composition), the aggregate consumption function is not simply an aggregate version of the individual consumption function (Hartley, 1997, p. 5). The next major development in macroeconomic discourse was the IS-LM model, proposed by John Hicks (1937) in order to place Keynes' theory into an equilibrium framework. The IS-LM model which became dominant in the first post-WWII decades was also lacking microfoundations (De Vroey & Malgrange, 2012).

[1] These assumptions also generate serious consequences for the role of money markets. For instance: "The combination of assumptions, when coupled with the trivialisation of risk and uncertainty in these supposedly stochastic models, and the linearisation techniques used in their solution, render money, credit and asset prices largely irrelevant (Muellbauer, 2010, p. 1).

[2] In a subsequent work, Friedman states that "the best approach to analysing aggregate change is from the top down—that is, analyzing the behaviour of aggregates and then perhaps supplementing that analysis with an examination of the determinants of how the aggregate is divided among components—or from the bottom up—that is, analyzing directly each component and constructing the aggregate as a sum of components ... Keynes, like me, was clearly in the top-down category" (Friedman, 1976, p. 316).

On the contrary, in Hall's random walk model of consumption, the form of the individual and aggregate equations is identical. The aggregate consumption function is derived by solving the individual's maximisation problem. Thus, Hall's model is rigorously derived from an optimisation problem at the level of the individual's objective function and constraints (Hall, 1978; Hartley, 1997; Pignalosa, 2021). It must be noted that Hall does not employ the notion of the representative agent in the form that it appears in the standard DSGE literature. Instead, the term 'consumer' is the one that he frequently employed in his model building (Hall, 1978).

However, the strive to construct secure microfoundations for macroeconomic models has long been a central goal of mainstream macroeconomists (Rizvi, 1994; Carroll, 2000; King, 2012).[3] Many authors agree that from the early 1970s onwards, the drive for macroeconomic models to have 'proper' microeconomic foundations became much more apparent (Janssen, 2008; Denis, 2016; Hands, 2017). As was seen in Chap. 6, Robert Lucas's judgements about Keynesian theory, which became known as the 'Lucas critique', was an extremely important factor for the drive towards microfoundations in contemporary mainstream macroeconomic modelling (Lucas, 1975; see also De Vroey, 2016). Microfoundations are usually understood as the search for a description of agent-level behaviour from which aggregate-level consequences could be derived. 'Proper' in this context means three basic characteristics: (1) All economic agents are rational in the sense that they maximise some kind of intertemporal objective function (utility or profit). (2) Agents form their expectations about the future in a rational way. (3) There is price and wage flexibility and all markets clear (Meeusen, 2011).

As was discussed previously, DSGE is the current dominant macroeconomic formulation, and it is synonymous with microfoundations. The importance of the microfoundations issue is very simply that modern mainstream macroeconomics is based entirely on DSGE models (Denis, 2016). Further, "general equilibrium theory is coextensive with the theory of the microfoundations of macroeconomics" (Weintraub, 1977, pp. 1–2).

The current dominance of DSGE modelling does not mean that it has been immune from serious criticisms by very influential figures. After

[3] For a history of microfoundations and its relationship to macroeconomics, see Backhouse and Boianovsky (2012); Duarte and Lima (2012).

Friedman's negative attitude to the need from microfoundations, James Tobin in a 2005 interview expressed his serious concerns:

> *Well, I think it's important for the behavioural equations of a macroeconomic model not to contradict choice-theoretic considerations, to be in principle consistent with them. But I think the stronger version of 'microfoundations' is a methodological mistake, one that has produced a tremendous amount of mischief.* (Snowdon & Vane, 2005, p. 153)

Working in the same Keynesian tradition as Tobin, William Baumol's stance is clearly negative: "I have little sympathy for efforts to provide extensive microeconomic foundations for macroeconomic analysis" (Baumol, 2009, p. 308). Other major figures associated with diverse strands of contemporary macroeconomics seem to converge on their views of microfoundations. David Laidler, for instance, criticised the microfoundations metaphor as an example of the 'Cartesian Fallacy' (Laidler, 1992, p. 104). Gregory Mankiw declared that "I am not sure that all macroeconomics necessarily has to start off with microeconomic building blocks" (Snowdon & Vane, 2005, p. 434). Robert Solow had expressed analogous negative views concerning microfoundations (Solow, 2008).[4]

Similarly, Oliver Blanchard has attacked DSGE modelling for its unrealistic microfoundations regarding the behaviour of households or, "assumptions profoundly at odds with what we know about consumers and firms" (Blanchard, 2016, p. 1). Hendry and Muellbauer identify a number of serious weaknesses of DSGE theory including the consumption Euler equation which is a key mechanism for the operation of model consistent-expectations, making it the main straitjacket of the representative agent DSGE approach (Hendry & Muellbauer, 2018, p. 303). Finally, Simon Wren-Lewis focuses on the wider costs of the "microfoundations hegemony", for both theory and policy:

> *This suggests that the microfoundations hegemony has had severe costs for macroeconomics, and could by implication have significant costs in the future. I would argue that ending the microfoundations hegemony is the most important step macroeconomists can take to improve their policy advice, and advance their discipline.* (Wren-Lewis, 2018, p. 55)

[4] For the negative views of other major macroeconomic theorists, see King (2012, pp. 173–187).

The Notion of Representative Agent

An essential component of microfoundations of the new classical macroeconomics is the notion of representative agent or household. The notion of the representative agent is the most indicative example of "Macroeconomists pursuing microfoundations for aggregate consumption" (Carroll, 2000, p. 110). The rise of the representative agent is almost parallel to the gradual emergence of the new neoclassical synthesis, better known nowadays as DSGE theory (Goodfriend & King, 1997; Hoover, 2012). In fact, the form of the representative agent model came into vogue with the rise of the new classical macroeconomics. It has become the predominant model in new classical work in general and real business cycle work in particular (Hartley, 1997, p. 6; see also Meeusen, 2011). The main reasons for its dominance are that representative agent models allow macroeconomic model-builders to avoid the Lucas critique, that they are a powerful means of constructing Walrasian (or general equilibrium) models, and that they are a means of providing microfoundations for macroeconomics (Hartley, 1997, p. 6). However, the notion of representative agent is a relatively recent development in macroeconomics given that the assumption has not traditionally been a part of Walrasian general equilibrium theory (Hands, 2017). Its origins as a concept can be traced back to Alfred Marshall's representative firm in his *Principles of Economics* (Marshall, 1920). It must be noted that the notion was abandoned mainly due to its severe criticism especially by Lionel Robbins and Allyn Young (see Hartley, 1997, pp. 9–18).[5]

The origin of the use of representative agent models in new classical macroeconomics is considered to be the Lucas and Rapping (1970) paper. In this paper, the authors set up a model in which a representative agent is used to determine the nature of labour supply. The representative household maximises utility based on current and future consumption and labour supply (see also Hartley, 1997). The use of the representative agent continued in Lucas' model of the business cycle (Lucas, 1975). Kydland and Prescott, and Long and Plosser also employed the representative agent notion in the process of development of the real business cycle theory (RBC) (Kydland & Prescott, 1977, 1982; Lucas & Prescott, 1979;

[5] For an extensive discussion of the origin and development of the notion of the representative agent as a component of microfoundations in twentieth century economics, see King (2012).

Long & Plosser, 1983; see also Meeusen, 2011). As was discussed in Chap. 7, the notion of the representative agent is still dominant in spite of the relatively recent emergence of agent heterogeneity in a number of relevant papers (Hands, 2017; Stiglitz, 2018, see also Chap. 7).

One of the fundamental points of criticism regarding the use of representative agent is the aggregation problem. For instance, James Hartley (1997) has argued that the representative agent models do not provide rigorous microfoundations and are neither a proper nor a particularly useful means of studying aggregate behaviour. Alan Kirman had pointed to the same problem:

> *Without any precise results on the relation between the properties of individual and aggregate demand behavior, the easiest way to proceed was simply to assume that the whole economy behaved as one individual.* (Kirman, 1992, p. 119)

Kirman concluded that "the assumption of a representative individual is far from innocent; it is the fiction by which macroeconomists can justify equilibrium analysis and provide pseudo-microfoundations" (Kirman, 1992, p. 125). Further and as has been pointed out by D. Wade Hands, it is only under very restrictive conditions that it is possible to add up the behaviour of a number of individually rational agents. In fact, starting with individual agents and aggregating them into a representative agent raises serious theoretical, empirical, and practical questions about aggregation given that each agent is characterised by different preferences and constraints (Hands, 2017, p. 1686).[6]

Very influential mainstream authors have also expressed serious reservations regarding the notion of representative agent. Kenneth Arrow, for instance, stated:

> *In particular, the homogeneity assumption seems to me to be especially dangerous. It denies the fundamental assumption of the economy, that it is built on gains from trading arising from individual differences. Further, it takes attention away from a very important aspect of the economy, namely, the effects of the distribution of income and of other individual characteristics on the workings of the economy.* (Arrow, 1986, p. 390)

[6] In more technical terms, all agents are assumed to have identical homothetic preferences (Hands, 2016).

In the same vein, Frank Hahn had argued explicitly against the use of the "representative agent as a disastrous concept" (Hahn, 1981; see also Hands, 2017, p. 1692).

As was mentioned in Chap. 8, James Tobin was very sceptical of the function of the representative agent. In a 2005 interview (cited above) and expressing the standard Keynesian thinking, Tobin was much more adamant against the use of concept, pointing out its negative role for macroeconomic theory:

> *I refer to the now orthodox requirement of postulating representative agents whose optimizations generate 'macroeconomic' behavioural equations. That is a considerable sacrifice of the essence of much of macroeconomics … It has put us on the wrong track in macroeconomics or what passes for macroeconomics.* (Snowdon & Vane, 2005, p. 155)

The criticism of the notion of the representative agent and in general of DSGE theory has been intensified after the emergence of the financial crisis of 2008, and by the failure of the theory to explain and predict the crisis as many leading economists have admitted (see also Rogers, 2014; Drakopoulos, 2016; Marchionatti & Sella, 2017). Axel Leijonhufvud supplied a forceful criticism:

> *I conclude that dynamic stochastic general equilibrium theory as an intellectually enterprise has been bankrupted by the crisis.* (Leijonhufvud, 2009, p. 755)

Finally, other well-known macroeconomic theorists such as Carroll (2000), Hoover (2001), De Grauwe (2010); Muellbauer (2016), and Stiglitz (2009, 2018) are among the many who have attacked the notion of the representative agent and its assumptions as a basis for macroeconomic modelling.

Methodological Individualism

The orthodox macroeconomics preoccupation with the establishment of microfoundations and the notion of representative agent can be largely attributed to methodological individualism, which is a core methodological component of mainstream economics (Hausman, 1992; Arrow, 1994; Taylor, 2004). As Maarten Janssen states: "The quest for microfoundations grew out of the widely felt, but rarely explicitly stated, desire to stick to the position of methodological individualism" (Janssen, 2008, p. 1). The influence of methodological individualism is not confined to orthodox macroeconomics. Most orthodox economists conceive economic interaction in terms of individual behaviour (see also Arrow, 1994; Udehn, 2002; Hodgson, 2007). As a result, the distinction between the individual and the social context holds, and the burden of explanation is usually placed on the individual. Further, there is a close connection between methodological individualism and the principal neoclassical assumptions (Arnsperger & Varoufakis, 2006; Nell & Errouaki, 2011).

Methodological individualism can be defined as "… the view that human social behaviour can be explained by understanding the behaviour of the individual decision-makers within a group" (Laing, 2011, p. 23). Further, methodological individualism in economics "appears to be based on an instinctive belief in *ontological individualism*: the doctrine that all that exists fundamentally for the economy are individual economic actors" (Hoover, 1995, p. 237, italics in original). The case of the representative agent is a clear demonstration of the central role of methodological individualism in contemporary formal macroeconomic models (see Denis, 2016). In particular and as Andy Denis writes: "the methodological individualism of modern, mainstream macroeconomics, embodied in the DSGE approach, is individualist in the extreme reductionist sense" (Denis, 2023, p. 23). Finally, it has been argued that methodological and ontological individualism facilitates the extensive use of mathematical modelling in mainstream economics (Lawson, 2012; Drakopoulos, 2025).

Despite its prominent status in the mainstream methodological framework, methodological individualism has been criticised by many influential economists, indicating that adhering to methodological individualism poses serious limitations for the study of economic phenomena.[7] Kenneth Arrow, for instance, argued:

> *I do conclude that social variables, not attached to particular individuals, are essential in studying the economy or any other social system.* (Arrow, 1994, p. 8)

In the same vein, John Davis agrees with Kenneth Arrow arguing that the idea of a genuinely isolated individual, free of all social relations, is

[7] For a general critique of the application of methodological individualism to social sciences, see Epstein (2015).

untenable (Davis, 2003, 2010). Geoffrey Hodgson provided a more general criticism:

> *However, as the examples of genes in biology and atomic particles in physics both illustrate, explanations in science are never in terms of micro-components alone: they always additionally involve interactive relations.* (Hodgson, 2007, p. 10)

Furthermore, well-known economic methodologists have been very critical of methodological individualism and of its implications for the field of macroeconomics.[8] In his early but much cited work, Mark Blaug considers the serious implications of the principle of methodological individualism:

> *In effect, it [methodological individualism] would rule out all macroeconomic propositions that cannot be reduced to microeconomic ones, and since few have yet been so reduced, this amounts in turn to saying goodbye to the whole of received macroeconomics. There must be something wrong with a methodological principle that has such devastating implications.* (Blaug, 1980, p. 51)

In agreement with Blaug, David Laidler maintained that "in the process of acquiring market-theoretic microfoundations, macroeconomics has lost its separate identity" (Laidler, 1990, p. 102). The effective 'disappearance' of macroeconomics is a view supported initially by Lucas, and more recently by other orthodox theorists (for a detailed discussion, see Taylor, 2004; Boumans & Davis, 2010).

Heterodox Macroeconomic Approaches

Given the previous discussion, we will provide a brief overview of the heterodox macroeconomics on the above issues. For most heterodox currents of macroeconomics, the methodological need for microfoundations of macroeconomics is nowhere near as it was observed in the orthodox macroeconomics analysis. As was seen in Chap. 8, Kalecki's economics was influenced by the approach of Classical political economy (e.g. the notion

[8] For instance, Marcel Boumans and John Davis (2010) view the claim that macroeconomics needs to have microfoundations, and should thereby be reduced to microeconomics, as an indicative example of reductionism. Instead, they defend a variety of pluralist positions in economics.

of socioeconomic classes). For Kalecki, the micro and the macro lie side by side interdependently, that is, on an equal footing (Kriesler, 1989, p. 136). Although Nicholas Kaldor did not make any direct references to the issue of microfoundations, his key notion of the increasing returns to scale, derived from Adam Smith and Allyn Young, was also explicitly macroeconomic (Chandra & Sandilands, 2010; see also King, 2012 for a more sceptical viewpoint). Luigi Pasinetti was clearly against the use of microfoundations, claiming that his position was shared not only by Kaldor but also by Robinson, Sraffa, and two other prominent 'Cambridge Keynesians', Richard Goodwin and Richard Kahn (Pasinetti, 2005, p. 843; see also King, 2012).

There are examples of many influential Post Keynesians who do not object to the idea of microfoundations for macroeconomics, and others who are ambivalent.[9] Paul Davidson and Malcolm Sawyer are two indicative examples who are not hostile to the idea. However, they are clearly opposed to the kind of microfoundations employed by orthodox economics. Davidson has always claimed that Post Keynesians are able to supply microfoundations for macroeconomic theory that are superior to those of the mainstream. He defends "the properties of a system of microeconomic demand and supply functions that has thrown out the axioms of ergodicity, ubiquitous gross substitution and non-neutral money" as the basis for a genuinely new Keynesian macroeconomics (Davidson, 2011, pp. 333–4). Although Sawyer argues that heterodox macroeconomics has always had microeconomic foundations, he is a very strong opponent of rational expectations—representative agent microfoundations. In his words:

> *Heterodox macroeconomics has not and would not wish to bring forward a universal set of microfoundations comparable to the manner in which the mainstream economists proceed. Heterodox macroeconomics has to grapple with the heterogeneity of behaviour and actions at the individual and organizational levels and with that behaviour in the context of fundamental uncertainty.* (Sawyer, 2010, p. 294)

The representative agent assumption is almost universally rejected by heterodox macroeconomists of the Post Keynesian line of thought. First of all, the questioning—to say the least—of the assumption of utility

[9] For a detailed discussion of the position of heterodox economists on this issue, see King (2012, chapter 8).

maximising agents is seen as a core distinguishing characteristic of most heterodox approaches. As Amitava Dutt maintains: "... the optimizing approach of neoclassical economics is important in distinguishing it from heterodox approaches" (Dutt, 2003, p. 59). Drawing from Keynes' critique of the expected utility maximisation model of mainstream theory, most Post Keynesian economists do not accept the construct of representative agent. Instead, they suggest an alternative approach to consumer choice (for a review, see Lavoie, 2022, pp. 75–127). Further, the central notion of fundamental uncertainty (discussed in Chap. 8) as opposed to the probability-based uncertainty of orthodox economics is another reason for the rejection of the expected utility maximising agents.

Other strands of heterodox economics have also expressed serious doubts regarding the methodological aspects of microfoundations and the related construct of the representative agent. Representing the intellectual tradition of Veblen ('Old Institutionalism'), Hodgson rejects the notion of utility maximising agents:

> *Institutionalism treats individuals not as fixed utility maximizers, but shaped by their institutional and cultural situations.* (Hodgson, 2000, p. 318)

In fact, he maintains that the above proposition "is a guiding thread through the whole institutionalist tradition, from Veblen to Galbraith" (Hodgson, 2000, pp. 318–319). Further, Hodgson has pointed to the general epistemological weakness of methodological individualism, including its shortcomings even in natural sciences (Hodgson, 2007). Hodgson's stance on this topic is not unique: "For institutionalists, the principal flaw of neoclassical thought is its 'methodological individualism,' which treats individuals as independent, self-sufficient beings with given preferences, while in reality individuals are culturally and mutually interdependent" (Ferrari-Filho & Conceição, 2005, p. 590). Similarly and following Veblen's consumption analysis, the Institutionalist David Hamilton rejects the standard theory of consumption as based on 'Bentham's felicific calculus', emphasising instead the social and institutional aspects of aggregate consumption (Hamilton, 1987; see also Todorova, 2014). In the same vein, other heterodox economists discard the orthodox consumption approach on similar grounds. For instance, Heilbroner and Milberg argue against New Classical economics, since it involves "a denial of the sociality not only of governments but of all economic agents and the markets in which they interact, and ignores questions of power, commitment and values" (Heilbroner & Milberg, 1995, pp. 83–84).

Concluding Comments

This chapter examined the methodological framework in which modern approaches to aggregate consumption are operating. Initially, it focused on the main strands of contemporary mainstream macroeconomics and distinguished their three fundamental components: the need for micro-foundations, the concept of representative agent, and methodological individualism. The main criticisms of those components were also presented. For comparison purposes, a brief overview of the heterodox macroeconomics on the above issues was also considered. In view of the discussion, it can be maintained that in mainstream models aggregate consumption is effectively reduced to the microeconomic theory of intertemporal choice. Contrary to pre-Keynesian, Keynesian, and many heterodox approaches, aggregate consumption has lost its 'aggregate' dimension. Effectively, it has been reduced to the intertemporal choice of an agent isolated from her/his social environment, interactions with other individuals and devoid of any other socio-economic characteristics which affect consumption decisions.

In the next and final chapter, we will turn to the economic policy implications of the various approaches to aggregate consumption that were discussed so far. Some general observations pertaining to the development of the theory of consumption in economics will also be drawn.

References

Arnsperger, C., & Varoufakis, Y. (2006). What Is Neoclassical Economics? The three Axioms Responsible for its Theoretical Oeuvre, Practical Irrelevance and, Thus, Discursive Power. *Panoeconomicus, 1*, 5–18.

Arrow, K. (1986). Rationality of Self and Others in an Economic System. *Journal of Business, 59*, 385–399.

Arrow, K. (1994). Methodological Individualism and Social Knowledge. *American Economic Review (Papers and Proceedings), 84*(2), 1–9.

Baumol, W. (2009). Endogenous Growth: Valuable Advance, Substantive Misnomer. In M. Boianovsky & K. D. Hoover (Eds.), *Robert Solow and the Development of Growth Economics* (pp. 304–314). Duke University Press.

Backhouse, R. & Boianovsky, M. (2012). *Transforming Modern Macroeconomics: Exploring Disequilibrium Microfoundations, 1956–2003.* Cambridge University Press.

Blanchard, O. (2016). Do DSGE Models Have a Future? *Policy Brief* 16–11, 1–4. Peterson Institute for International Economics.

Blaug, M. (1968). *Economic Theory in Retrospect* (2nd ed.). Heinemann.

Blaug, M. (1980). *The Methodology of Economics.* Cambridge University Press.

Boumans, M., & Davis, J. (2010). *Economic Methodology: Understanding Economics as a Science.* Palgrave Macmillan.

Carroll, C. (2000). Requiem for the Representative Consumer? Aggregate Implications of Microeconomic Consumption Behavior. *American Economic Review Papers and Proceedings, 90*(2), 110–115.

Carroll, C. (2001). A Theory of the Consumption Function, with and without Liquidity Constraints. *Journal of Economic Perspectives, 15*(3), 23–45.

Chandra, R., & Sandilands, R. (2010). Reply to Roy H. Grieve on Increasing Returns. *Review of Political Economy, 22*(1), 141–150.

Chick, V., & Jespersen, J. (2023). Holism and the Fallacy of Composition in Macroeconomics. In J. Jespersen, V. Chick, & B. Tieben (Eds.), *Routledge Handbook of Macroeconomic Methodology* (pp. 54–63). Routledge.

Davidson, P. (2011). *Post Keynesian Macroeconomic Theory: A Foundation for Successful Economic Policies for the Twenty-First Century.* 2nd Edition, Edward Elgar Publishing.

Davis, J. (2003). *The Theory of the Individual in Economics.* Cambridge University Press.

Davis, J. (2010). *Individuals and Identity in Economics.* Cambridge University Press.

De Grauwe, P. (2010). The Scientific Foundation of Dynamic Stochastic General Equilibrium (DSGE) Models. *Public Choice, 144*, 413–433.

De Vroey, M. (2016). *A History of Macroeconomics from Keynes to Lucas and Beyond.* Cambridge University Press.

De Vroey, M., & Malgrange, P. (2012). From the 'Keynesian Revolution' to the Klein-Goldberger Model: Klein and the Dynamization of Keynesian Theory. *History of Economic Ideas, 20*(2), 113–135.

Denis, A. (2016). Microfoundations. *Review of Political Economy, 28*(1), 134–152.

Denis, A. (2023). Methodological Individualism and Macroeconomics. In J. Jespersen, V. Chick, & B. Tieben (Eds.), *Routledge Handbook of Macroeconomic Methodology* (pp. 15–24). Routledge.

Drakopoulos, S. A. (2016). Economic Crisis, Economic Methodology and the Scientific Ideal of Physics. *Journal of Philosophical Economics, 10*(1), 28–57.

Drakopoulos, S. A. (2025). The Conceptual Resilience of the Atomistic Individual in Mainstream Economic Rationality. *Review of Political Economy, 37*(1), 1–20.

Duarte, P. (2012). Not Going Away? Microfoundations in the Making of a New Consensus in Macroeconomics. In P. Duarte & G. Lima, G. (eds)

Microfoundations Reconsidered: The Relationship of Micro and Macroeconomics in Historical Perspective (pp. 190–238). Edward Elgar Publishing.

Duarte, P., & Lima, G. (Eds.). (2012) *Microfoundations Reconsidered: The Relationship of Micro and Macroeconomics in Historical Perspective.* Edward Elgar.

Dutt, A. (2003). On Post Walrasian Economics, Macroeconomic Policy, and Heterodox Economics. *International Journal of Political Economy, 33*(2), 47–67.

Eichengreen, B. (2020). Keynesian Economics: Can It Return If It Never Died? *Review of Keynesian Economics, 8*(1), 23–35.

Epstein, B. (2015). *The Ant Trap: Rebuilding the Foundations of the Social Sciences.* Oxford University Press.

Ferrari-Filho, F., & Conceição, O. (2005). The Concept of Uncertainty in Post Keynesian Theory and in Institutional Economics. *Journal of Economic Issues, 39*(3), 579–594.

Friedman, M. (1957). *The Consumption Function.* Princeton University Press.

Friedman, M. (1976). "Comment" [on Tobin and Buiter]. In J. L. Stein (Ed.), *Monetarism* (pp. 310–317). North-Holland.

Goodfriend, M., & King, R. (1997). The new Neoclassical Synthesis and the Role of Monetary Policy. In B. Bernanke & J. Rotemberg (Eds.), *NBER Macroeconomics Annual 1997* (pp. 231–296). MIT Press.

Hahn, F. (1981). *Money and Inflation.* MIT Press.

Hall, R. E. (1978). Stochastic Implications of the Life Cycle-Permanent Income Hypothesis: Theory and Evidence. *Journal of Political Economy, 86*(6), 971–987.

Hamilton, D. (1987). Institutional Economics and Consumption. *Journal of Economic Issues, 21*(4), 1531–1554.

Hands, W. (2016). The Individual and the Market: Paul Samuelson on (Homothetic) Santa Claus economics. *European Journal of the History of Economic Thought, 23*, 425–452.

Hands, W. (2017). Conundrums of the Representative Agent. *Cambridge Journal of Economics, 41*, 1685–1704.

Hartley, J. (1997). *The Representative Agent in Macroeconomics.* Routledge.

Hausman, D. (1992). *The Inexact and Separate Science of Economics.* Cambridge University Press.

Heilbroner, R., & Milberg, W. (1995). *The Crisis of Vision in Modern Economic Thought.* Cambridge University Press.

Hendry, D., & Muellbauer, J. (2018). The Future of Macroeconomics: Macro Theory and Models at the Bank of England. *Oxford Review of Economic Policy, 34*(1–2), 287–328.

Hicks, J. (1937). Mr. Keynes and the 'Classics'. *Econometrica, 5*, 147–159.

Hodgson, G. (2000). What Is the Essence of Institutional Economics? *Journal of Economic Issues, 34*(2), 317–329.

Hodgson, G. (2007). Meanings of Methodological Individualism. *Journal of Economic Methodology, 14*(2), 211–226.
Hoover, K. (1995). Is Macroeconomics for Real? *The Monist, 78*(3), 235–257.
Hoover, K. (2001). Does Macroeconomics Need Microfoundations? In K. D. Hoover (Ed.), *The Methodology of Empirical Macroeconomics* (pp. 57–89). Cambridge University Press.
Hoover, K. (2012). Microfoundational Programs. In P. G. Duarte & G. T. Lima (Eds.), *Microfoundations Reconsidered: The Relationship of Micro and Macroeconomics in Historical Perspective* (pp. 19–61). Edward Elgar.
Janssen, M. (2008). Microfoundations. In S. N. Durlauf & L. E. Blume (Eds.), *The New Palgrave: A Dictionary of Economics* (2nd ed., pp. 1–10). Palgrave Macmillan.
Jespersen, J. (2009). *Macroeconomic Methodology: A Post-Keynesian Perspective.* Edward Elgar.
Keynes, J. M. (1936). *The General Theory of Employment, Interest, and Money.* Macmillan.
King, J. (2012). *The Microfoundations Delusion: Metaphor and Dogma in the History of Macroeconomics.* Edward Elgar.
Kirman, A. (1992). Whom or What Does the Representative Individual Represent? *Journal of Economic Perspectives, 6*, 117–136.
Kriesler, P. (1989). Methodological implications of Kalecki's microfoundations. In M. Sebastiani (Ed.), *Kalecki's Relevance Today* (pp. 121–141). Macmillan.
Kydland, F. E., & Prescott, E. C. (1977). Rules rather than Discretion: the inconsistency of optimal plans. *Journal of Political Economy, 85*, 473–491.
Kydland, F. E., & Prescott, E. C. (1982). Time to Build and Aggregate Fluctuations. *Econometrica, 50*, 1345.
Laidler, D. (1990). *Taking Money Seriously and Other Essays.* Philip Allan.
Laidler, D. (1992). The Cycle before New Classical Economics. In M. T. Belongia & M. R. Garfinkel (Eds.), *The Business Cycle: Theories and Evidence* (pp. 85–112). Kluwer.
Laing, D. (2011). *Labour Economics: Introduction to Classic and the New Labour Economics.* Norton.
Lavoie, M. (2022). *Post-Keynesian Economics: New Foundations* (2nd ed.). Edward Elgar.
Lawson, T. (2012). Mathematical Modelling and Ideology in the Economics Academy: Competing Explanations of the Failings of the Modern Discipline? *Economic Thought, 1*, 3–22.
Leijonhufvud, A. (2009). Out of the Corridor: Keynes and the Crisis. *Cambridge Journal of Economics, 33*(4), 741–757.
Long, J., Jr., & Plosser, C. (1983). Real Business Cycles. *Journal of Political Economy, 91*, 39–69.

Lucas, R. (1975). An Equilibrium Model of the Business Cycle. *Journal of Political Economy, 83*, 1113–1144.

Lucas, R., & Prescott, E. (1979). Investment under Uncertainty. *Econometrica, 39*, 659–682.

Lucas, R., & Rapping, L. (1970). Real Wages, Employment and Inflation. In E. S. Phelps (Ed.), *Microeconomic Foundations of Employment and Inflation Theory* (pp. 257–305). W. W. Norton.

Marchionatti, R., & Sella, L. (2017). Is Neo-Walrasian Macroeconom(etr)ics a Dead End? An Assessment of Recent Criticisms of DSGE Models. *Journal of Post Keynesian Economics, 40*(4), 441–469.

Marshall, A. (1920). [1961]). *Principles of Economics*, 9th [variorum] edition with annotations by C. W. Guillebaud, 2 vols. Macmillan.

Meeusen, W. (2011). Whither the Microeconomic Foundations of Macroeconomic Theory ? *Brussels Economic Review, 54*(1), 51–80.

Muellbauer, J. (2010). *Household Decisions, Credit Markets and the Macroeconomy: Implications for the Design of Central Bank Models.* Bank for International Settlements Discussion Paper 306, March 2010, pp.1–60.

Muellbauer, J. (2016). *Macroeconomics and Consumption.* Economics Series Working Papers Paper, No. 811, University of Oxford, Department of Economics, Oxford, UK, pp. 1–37.

Nell, E., & Errouaki, K. (2011). *Rational Econometric Man.* Edward Elgar.

Pasinetti, L. L. (2005). The Cambridge School of Keynesian Economics. *Cambridge Journal of Economics, 29*(6), 837–848.

Pignalosa, D. (2021). The Euler Equation Approach: Critical Implications of Recent Developments in the Theory of Intertemporal Choice. *Bulletin of Political Economy, 15*(1), 1–43.

Rizvi, S. (1994). The Microfoundations Project in General Equilibrium Theory. *Cambridge Journal of Economics, 18*(4), 357–377.

Rogers, C. (2014). Why 'State of the Art' Monetary Theory was Unable to Anticipate the Global Financial Crisis: A Child's Guide. *European Journal of Economics and Economic Policies Intervention, 11*(3), 300–314.

Sawyer, M. (2010). Crises and Paradigms in Macroeconomics. *Intervention. European Journal of Economics and Economic Policies, 7*(2), 283–302.

Snowdon, B., & Vane, H. (2005). *Modern Macroeconomics: Its Origins, Development and Current State.* Edward Elgar.

Solow, R. (2008). The State of Macroeconomics. *Journal of Economic Perspectives, 22*(1), 243–246.

Stiglitz, J. (2009). The Current Economic Crisis and Lessons for Economic Theory. *Eastern Economic Journal, 35*(3), 281–296.

Stiglitz, J. (2018). Where Modern Macroeconomics Went Wrong. *Oxford Review of Economic Policy, 34*(1–2), 70–106.

Taylor, L. (2004). *Reconstructing Macroeconomics: Structuralist Proposals and Critiques of the Mainstream*. Harvard University Press.

Todorova, Z. (2014). Consumption as a Social Process. *Journal of Economic Issues, 48*(3), 663–678.

Udehn, L. (2002). The Changing Face of Methodological Individualism. *Annual Review of Sociology, 28*, 479–507.

Weintraub, E. R. (1977). The Microfoundations of Macroeconomics: A Critical Survey. *Journal of Economic Literature, 15*(1), 1–23.

Wren-Lewis, S. (2018). Ending the Microfoundations Hegemony. *Oxford Review of Economic Policy, 34*(1–2).

CHAPTER 10

Policy Implications and Conclusions

Introduction

The purpose of this final chapter is to provide an overview of the material discussed in the previous chapters with particular emphasis on the economic policy implications of the various consumption functions. In the discussion so far, the important issue of the economic policy implications was mentioned but not explored in detail. Different approaches to aggregate consumption imply important consequences for the role and effectiveness of economic policy. The absolute and relative income hypotheses of consumption offered strong theoretical foundations for activist fiscal policy. In contrast, the life-cycle and permanent-income hypotheses undermined the theoretical justification of the key role of fiscal policy in economic stabilisation. The case for non-activist economic policy was strengthened further with the modern versions of consumption function based on Euler's equation. Fiscal policy has no effect on inflation or output in the representative agent formulations of contemporary orthodox macroeconomic models. Generally, it can be argued that the introduction of rational (in the mainstream sense) agents seriously weakened the strong policy results arising from Keynes' and Duesenberry's approaches, including those from heterodox consumption theories which do not depend on the above notion.

This chapter will start with a summary of the policy implications emerging from the consumption formulations of Keynes, Duesenberry, and

S. A. Drakopoulos, *The Consumption Function in Economics*, https://doi.org/10.1007/978-3-032-15958-8_10

Keynesianism. It will proceed with the economic policy consequences of mainstream theories based on rational forward-looking optimising agents. It will then discuss the policy implications of Old or standard Keynesianism, Post Keynesian consumption formulations, other heterodox schools, and non-mainstream strands such as the new behavioural economics. The presence of ideological considerations in policy recommendations will also be briefly discussed. A general conclusion summarising the main arguments of this book will close the chapter.

Keynes, Duesenberry, and Keynesianism

Apart from the academic dimension, the theoretical analysis of aggregate consumption patterns has very important economic policy consequences. Aggregate consumption largely determines the effectiveness of fiscal policy for economic stabilisation. In Keynes and in the standard Keynesian analysis, consumption depends on current income. In turn, the marginal propensity to consume determines the magnitudes of government expenditure and tax multipliers. It also determines the magnitude of the private investment multiplier. This suggests that the effectiveness of fiscal policy—that is, changes in taxation and government spending—to smooth out economic downturns, and thus large fluctuations of produced output and employment, is closely linked to the level of fiscal multipliers, and therefore to the nature of the consumption function. As was seen in Chap. 3, the larger the MPC, the larger the multiplier effect. In other words, the effects of fiscal policy depend on the marginal propensity to consume (MPC) out of shocks to income. Thus, consumption is fundamental in Keynes and in Keynesian macroeconomics (see Bunting, 1989; Boug et al., 2021). In this theoretical framework, fiscal policy is very powerful, especially in times of economic downturns. In an economic downturn, the presence of the liquidity trap is likely to render monetary policy ineffective. Further and according to Keynes, the government expenditure multiplier is higher in absolute terms than the tax multiplier, and this means that government expenditure is important in recessions, and extremely important in economic depressions (Skidelsky, 1992; Dow, 2023).

An essential component of Keynes' and Keynesian consumption analysis is that MPC is less than APC. This inequality also supports the case for progressive taxation as an instrument of income redistribution, given that the transfer of income from high-income groups to low-income consumers will raise the level of aggregate demand and the level of income

(Bunting, 1989; Krueger, 2012). Further, as households spend a decreasing share of their incomes as society becomes richer (at the margin), a greater proportion of investment will be required to maintain full-employment income levels. In general, the role of fiscal policy is crucial not only for economic stabilisation but also for income redistribution and for maintaining long-run full employment (Dow, 2023).

As in the Keynesian framework, similar economic policy implications arise from the relative income hypothesis, given that the APC will be greater than the MPC (Kosobud, 1998, p. 135). Furthermore, Duesenberry's approach implies a subtler role of taxation policy than in the Keynesian framework. Tax policy is more efficient in the case of recessions than in an expansionary phase. Although tax reductions may well stimulate consumption spending, tax increases may not have a significant effect in curbing demand in the short-run (Duesenberry, 1949, pp. 96–102; Kosicki, 1990; Alvarez-Cuadrado & Long, 2011). Additionally, the positional goods character of relative consumption may substantially increase the optimal marginal tax rate, and that may induce significantly more redistribution, creating a further incentive for income redistribution from wealthy to poor citizens (Boskin & Sheshinski, 1978; McCormick, 2018). Finally and under consumption interdependency, progressive taxation for explicit redistributive purposes may be fully consistent with the Pareto criterion (Postlewaite, 1998; Corneo, 2002; Truyts, 2010).

Mainstream Theories Based on Rational Optimising Agents

As has been stated before, the emergence of consumption theories based on rational forward-looking agents undermined the theoretical effectiveness of fiscal policy. In the consumption analysis by Modigliani and Brumberg life-cycle model, fiscal policy and especially taxation policy is much less effective. Tax reduction has a smaller impact compared to the Keynesian consumption function, since tax cuts are smoothed and spent over an individual's entire remaining lifespan (Bunting, 2001; Drakopoulos, 2021). Further, changes in current income arising from fiscal policy will have a strong effect on current consumption only if they affect expected lifetime income (see also Jappelli & Pistaferri, 2014). The key policy implication here is that the framework of life-cycle hypothesis provides much less theoretical support for active fiscal policy in comparison to the absolute and relative income hypotheses.

Friedman's permanent-income hypothesis reaches similar results to life-cycle theory. If consumption is proportional to permanent income, the power of tax-induced changes in aggregate demand is significantly reduced (Friedman, 1957, p. 238). As Lance Taylor observed: "...in Friedman's world the permanent income hypothesis makes demand multipliers vanish, fiscal policy is weak in both the short and the long runs" (Taylor, 2004, p. 207). Apart from the inefficiency of fiscal policy in raising output in the long-run, the basic policy message of Monetarism was the central role of monetary policy in controlling inflation. It should also be kept in mind that the rise of Monetarism was initially the main form of reaction against Keynesian-based economic policies. Monetarism was largely grounded on Friedman's consumption function and on his quantity theory of money (Friedman, 1956). In terms of general policy implications, both life-cycle and permanent-income theories of consumption seriously undermined the Keynesian case for activist fiscal policy (Snowdon & Vane, 2005, p. 195).

As was seen in Chap. 7, the introduction of rational expectations into the consumption function further weakened the role of activist economic policy. The original formulations of the random walk theory of consumption implied that traditional Keynesian demand management mainly through fiscal policy will have virtually no effect on real consumption. More specifically, if expectations concerning income are fully rational (taking into account all available information about the future), then consumption should not depend on a weighted average of past income but will, instead, follow a random walk (Hall, 1978). In the context of the Euler equation, a change in income or wealth that was anticipated has already been factored into expected permanent income, so that it will not change consumption. Thus, the rational expectation model denies any intended and systematic impact of the policy-makers' tools on very important macroeconomic indicators such as output and employment (Marchionatti & Sella, 2017; Foster, 2021). This policy view was further reinforced by the introduction of Ricardian equivalence where perfectly rational households fully anticipate changes in Government's actions (i.e. shifts between debt and tax finance for a given amount of public expenditure), and adjust their behaviour accordingly (Barro, 1979). The clear policy implication was that fiscal policy is completely ineffective in raising aggregate demand and output.

Contemporary mainstream macroeconomic models, such as the DSGE and particularly the RANK versions, reach similar conclusions concerning economic policy. In these models, the role of economic policy is also very limited, given that policy changes will affect consumption only if they are not anticipated. Further, in the majority of the RANK models, households are assumed to be fully insured against idiosyncratic shocks (e.g. Gali, 2015). In most of these models, fiscal policy has no effect on inflation or output also because of Ricardian equivalence. Instead, monetary policy plays the lead role in stabilisation, as the central bank uses interest rate cuts (increases) to offset the effects of adverse (positive) demand shocks (Kocherlakota, 2022). There is a long-standing consensus that macroeconomic stabilisation should rely on monetary policy, not fiscal policy.

As was argued in Chap. 9, the failure to predict and to explain the financial crisis of 2008 led a number of influential macroeconomists to re-examine the assumptions and the structure of the standard DSGE models. Central components of the orthodox macroeconomic theory such as the core assumption that markets clear continuously were also questioned (e.g. Laidler, 2010; Muellbauer, 2016). Furthermore, the crisis brought renewed interest in how household asset composition, liquidity, and credit market conditions may affect consumption patterns (Boug et al., 2021). The emergence of TANK and HANK formulations with heterogeneity-augmented households can be viewed as a result of the criticism induced by the financial crisis. The very interesting aspect of those formulations is that their policy implications are not far from the old Keynesian ones. In particular, key mechanisms of many of those models point to the revival of concepts such as 'The Keynesian cross', the marginal propensity to consume (MPC), and monetary and fiscal multipliers (e.g. Kaplan et al., 2018; Bilbiie, 2020; Kocherlakota, 2022; Andrés, 2024). Further, the presence of habits and following behaviour such as the 'keeping up with the Joneses' also point to a much stronger role for fiscal policy with strong multiplier effects, and therefore to the traditional Keynesian demand management policies (e.g. Bernasconi et al., 2020). There are also empirical works that indicate that the size of the MPC is much larger than what used to be common in many standard DSGE models (Boug et al., 2021).[1] For instance, Carroll and his colleagues introduce a modest degree of

[1] Earlier empirical evidence suggested that short-term multipliers are positive, ranging from 0.1 to 3.1, with expenditure multipliers being in the range of 0.6 to 1.4, and tax multipliers in the range of 0.3 to 0.8 (Hemming et al., 2002).

heterogeneity in household preferences or beliefs in their model. They predict an aggregate MPC of around 20% compared to roughly 5% implied by macroeconomic models with representative agents (Carroll et al., 2017). In general and especially after the coronavirus pandemic, an increasing number of macroeconomists appear to take a very different view on fiscal policy, recommending an active fiscal policy stance and even an increase in debt-to-GDP levels (Heise, 2023).

Old Keynesianism, Post Keynesians, and Other Heterodox Schools

As was discussed in Chap. 8, Tobin's work can be viewed as representing the 'old' or standard Keynesian analysis. Operating mainly in the IS-LM analytical framework, Tobin's stance on economic policy is supportive of activist monetary and fiscal policy. For instance, Tobin held that there is statistically significant interest-responsiveness of money demand and this means that there was a distinct role for fiscal policy in stabilisation policy (e.g. Tobin, 1956). In general, the key conclusions from his works were very supportive of the effectiveness of fiscal policy for aggregate demand management (see also Buiter, 2003). Tobin also engaged in an academic debate with Milton Friedman arguing against Friedman's Monetarism and its policy and especially, its fiscal policy implications (e.g. Tobin, 1972). Further, he rejected the real business cycle literature conclusions regarding the ineffectiveness of activist economic policy (e.g. Kydland & Prescott, 1982; see also Buiter, 2003).

The Post Keynesian approach exhibits some fundamental differences in comparison to the mainstream.[2] Following the Kalecki-Kaldor-Pasinetti line of thought, Post Keynesians are often deeply concerned with distributional issues rather than with economic efficiency. They also recognise the importance of aggregate demand policies (e.g. Dutt, 2003). Further, the focus on the Keynesian notion of fundamental uncertainty

[2] Louis-Philippe Rochon lists the following characteristics that appear in the description of post-Keynesian economics by various authors: (1) realism or the need to reflect the 'real world', (2) a monetary theory of production and endogenous money, (3) the importance of social classes and power, (4) economies are characterised by instability and fragility, (5) the principle of effective demand is central to understanding output and growth, (6) the importance of income distribution, (7) the essential nature of involuntary unemployment; (8) uncertainty and historical time are important to economic analysis; (9) institutions are important; (10) fiscal policy dominance (Rochon, 2023, pp. 266–67 and references therein).

means that the orthodox formulations of rational forward-looking optimising consumers are not accepted. As was seen in chapter 8, fundamental uncertainty leads households to put more savings in liquid assets. In addition, there is an inverse relationship between changes in the MPC and fundamental uncertainty, and this implies the existence of precautionary saving motive (e.g. Menz, 2010). Consequently, fiscal policy remains a powerful instrument of regulating the level of aggregate demand. Fiscal policy is seen as a key policy tool when the economy needs aggregate demand boosting, and when the economy's resources are underutilised (Fazzari, 1994–1995; Arestis & Sawyer, 2003). For instance, in the case of expansionary fiscal policy, tax cuts on wages have a much stronger effect compared with tax cuts on profits (e.g. Blecker, 2025). In opposition to orthodox policy conclusions, deficit-financed government expenditure is considered as an important weapon against demand-deficient unemployment (King, 2013; Hein, 2023; Heise, 2023).

The social and institutional significance of consumption is the common idea that can be discerned in other strands of heterodox economics. A large part of this literature is utilising and expanding Veblen's approach to consumption (e.g. Hamilton, 1987; Todorova, 2014). John Kenneth Galbraith's analysis of consumption can be viewed as an example of this strand. Galbraith paid particular attention to exploring how advertising and consumer credit help drive consumption patterns. Although not stated explicitly, it seems that he endorsed a Keynesian consumption function with consumption being a function of disposable income, augmented with aggregate advertising and consumer credit as two extra variables (Galbraith, 1958; for a detailed discussion, see Lamdin, 2008). Reflecting the Keynesian macroeconomic policy thinking of his time, he was a proponent of increased taxes at the personal level to achieve redistribution and social balance. Galbraith was also in favour of increased government spending for public needs of the highest importance (Galbraith, 1958; Galbraith, 1967, p. 57; Lamdin, 2008, p. 607).

New Behavioural Economics

Although the new behavioural economics stream of thought does not belong to the heterodox tradition, one can find important criticisms of the orthodox approach regarding consumption, saving, and the ensuing economic policies.[3] The new behavioural economics emerged, mainly, in the well-known contributions of Kahneman and Tversky (1979), Thaler (1980) and their followers, who aimed at behaviourally improving, rather than replacing, consumer choice theory (Edwards, 2014, p. 716; also Sent, 2004). Notions such as reference dependence, loss aversion, adaptation, endowment effects, and framing effects are part of their criticism of the mainstream rational agent model (Rabin, 2002; Earl, 2018). The criticism has also important consequences for aggregate consumption and savings patterns.

Richard Thaler's work (i.e. 1980, 2015) can be viewed as a new behavioural economics representative. Thaler emphasises both the significance of limits to human capacities for self-control and the tendency for people to select default options and fail to take long-term perspectives. For instance, Thaler has serious concerns about the potential for home-equity mortgages to result in people ending up going into retirement without having paid off their mortgages. Further, people might have poor appreciation of compound interest and tendencies towards hyperbolic discounting/present bias (Earl, 2022, pp. 400–403). As Peter Earl points out: "The retirement saving issue has been one of Thaler's long-standing interests because of his concern with weakness of will, loss aversion and status quo bias" (Earl, 2018, p. 116). In general, the issue of under-saving pattern is explained by employing the notions of loss aversion and present bias (meaning that extra weight is given to current payoffs), thus diverting from the rational choice model (Barberis, 2018). The notions can be connected to his critique of lifetime/permanent income perspectives via his theoretical construction of 'mental accounting' which incorporates basic parts of Thaler's ideas (1999). For instance, mental accounting might cause the marginal propensity to consume to vary significantly based on the source of income: windfall income and inheritance income have different MPC compared to regular earned income. (Shefrin & Thaler, 1988). Referring to the predictions of his mental accounting model, Thaler declares:

[3] For many specialists, old behavioural economics (e.g. Leibnstein, Katona, Simon) is much further from orthodox economics compared to the new or modern behavioural economics (e.g. Kahneman, Tversky, Thaler) (see, for instance, Sent, 2004; Edwards, 2014; Frantz, 2020).

> *These predictions are in sharp contrast to standard economic theory of saving: the life-cycle model (Modigliani and Brumberg, 1954;* Friedman, 1957*).* (Thaler, 1999, p. 196)

More generally, in Thaler's view the traditional model of intertemporal choice fails to capture some basic aspects of economic behaviour, and therefore it has serious implications for the orthodox consumption theories based on rational optimising agents.

The Presence of Ideology

The discussion of historical development of consumption functions indicated that the ideological dimension was an important element in the displacement of the Keynesian consumption function. It is very likely that ideological considerations are also present in contemporary mainstream macroeconomics, including formulations regarding aggregate consumption. For instance, the persistence of microfoundations and of the construct of representative agent has been characterised as "dogma" (e.g. King, 2012). Kevin Hoover openly refers to the ideology of microfoundations. As he writes: "My contention is that, even in its neutral sense, the ideology of microfoundations rests on a mistake about the ontology of the social world; whereas, in its pejorative sense, it shares the characteristic, common to political ideologies, of serving as a tool of persecution and intellectual repression" (Hoover, 2009, p. 388).

Some major figures in macroeconomics have explicitly attributed a political or ideological dimension regarding the general debate on economic policy. Tobin, for instance, argued that the Monetarist counter-revolution against Keynesian aggregate demand policies, which started gaining momentum in the 1970s, was also assisted by the rise of conservative ideologies (Tobin, 1981; see also Trezzini, 2012). Apart from Monetarism, new classical macroeconomics were assessed in terms of a certain political ideology. As Tobin wrote:

> *This is a more fundamental theme than the technical sovereignty of any monetary aggregate and it is more congenial to free enterprise ideology. It is also the theme of the second wave of the monetarist counter-revolution, the new classical macro-economics. The new doctrine has given a theoretical rationale for propositions that were previously matters of faith and empirical judgement. The grasp of the Invisible Hand is extended beyond micro-economic resource alloca-*

> *tion to macro-economic optimality – market competition produces not just a tendency towards long-run optima but a continuous sequence of equilibria.* (Tobin, 1981, p. 35)

The strong bias towards the superiority of the free markets and the ensuing policy advice has also been identified by other studies (e.g. Keen, 2011; Lepers, 2017; Heise, 2022). Almost three decades later, Robert Solow evaluates modern mainstream macroeconomic theory in rather similar terms:[4]

> *Moreover it[modern macroeconomic theory] is practically guaranteed to give laissez-faire-type advice, which happens to fit nicely with the general turn to the political right that began in the 1970s and may or may not be coming to an end.* (Solow, 2008, p. 245)

The role of ideology in the formation of economic theory is a complicated and contested issue with a long presence in the history of economic thought (see the classic work by Hutchison, 1964; see also Backhouse, 2010 and references therein). The history of the consumption function indicated that the political ideology dimension was, and still is, present in consumption theories.[5]

General Conclusions

This short monograph attempted to investigate the methodological and policy implications of the notion of consumption function in economics discourse. To a large extent, it followed an historical approach with emphasis on the major developments and turning points of the consumption function studies. It was argued that the first theories of aggregate consumption assigned a significant role to the psychological and sociological dimensions on consumption decisions, culminating in Keynes' absolute

[4] According to Solow, the term *modern macroeconomics* means: "…a macroeconomics that is deduced from a model in which a single immortal consumer–worker–owner maximizes a perfectly conventional time-additive utility function over an infinite horizon, under perfect foresight or rational expectations, and in an institutional and technological environment that favors universal price-taking behavior" (Solow, 2008, p. 243).

[5] The role of ideological influences on economic theory is part of the general epistemological issue of the relationship between science and political ideology (see, for instance, Mantzavinos, 2024 and references therein).

income hypothesis. After a short period of dominance, Keynes' consumption function was gradually displaced by consumption functions such as the life-cycle and the permanent-income hypotheses based on utility maximising and forward-looking consumers. This change represented a paradigmatic shift in the study of consumption because it was grounded on an entirely different methodological framework. The need for microfoundations for macroeconomic theory, the notion of representative agent and methodological individualism were the pillars of this framework expressed mainly in the DSGE constructions. Thus, the orthodox formulations that followed became much more anchored to the assumption of optimising agents with rational expectations. They were supplemented with the standard additional assumptions of an environment of calculable risk and agent homogeneity.

Overall, there was a clearly discernable move away from consumption theories which recognised the social significance of consumption and its psychological dimensions, to theories based on the conception of isolated rational consumers with no social influences and interactions. The work also presented the main heterodox consumption theories as a way of comparison with the mainstream. Heterodox approaches to consumption criticised the core assumptions and the underlying methodological framework of mainstream consumption functions. We also observed criticisms targeting the core assumption of the rational agent originating from non-mainstream strands such as the new behavioural economics. The alternative theories preserve the social and psychological dimensions of consumption decisions, or adopt the notion of social classes instead of the socially isolated representative agent.

The methodological paradigm-shift also brought very different economic policy prescriptions than the ones promoted by standard Keynesian theory. The life-cycle and the permanent-income hypotheses implied smaller multipliers and diminished the effectiveness of fiscal policy. In the context of the ensuing Euler equation-based consumption theories, fiscal multipliers became non-significant and active fiscal policy was therefore completely undermined. However, the validity of these models (especially after the great recession of 2008) has been questioned even by leading mainstream theorists in terms of unrealistic microeconomic foundations regarding the behaviour of agents/households.

It is hoped that this study pointed to the paramount role of the underlying methodological framework in the development and formation of consumption theories.[6] The methodological framework does not only consist of the assumptions with respect to agents, but also of the whole environment in which agents operate, and of the choice of assumptions with their inevitable ideological connotations. Vitally related to the methodological framework are the economic policy implications arising from consumption theories. The study indicated that once the social and psychological dimension of consumption patterns is removed, the effectiveness of fiscal policy is greatly undermined. Socially isolated consumers with uniform and simplistic 'psychological' characteristics render fiscal policy almost worthless. However and even in the rather narrow framework of orthodoxy, the introduction of agent heterogeneity in consumption formulations revive the effectiveness of fiscal policy. The same holds with the introduction of a more realistic agent behavioural characteristics such as the presence of habits and following behaviour. In general, the present work could also be viewed as an additional case study of the central role of the methodological framework in economics discourse, and its strong influence on the debate regarding the selection of economic policies.

References

Alvarez-Cuadrado, F., & Long, N. V. (2011). The Relative Income Hypothesis. *Journal of Economic Dynamics and Control, 35*, 1489–1501.

Andrés, J. (2024). The Effectiveness of Fiscal Policy. In E. Alberola (Ed.), *Fiscal Policy in a Turbulent Era* (pp. 86–102). Edward Elgar.

Arestis, P., & Sawyer, M. (2003). Reinventing Fiscal Policy. *Journal of Post Keynesian Economics, 2*(1), 3–26.

Backhouse, R. (2010). *The Puzzle of Modern Economics: Science or Ideology?* Cambridge University Press.

Barberis, N. (2018). Richard Thaler and the Rise of Behavioral Economics. *Scandinavian Journal of Economics, 120*(3), 661–684.

Barro, R. (1979). On the Determination of the Public Debt. *Journal of Political Economy, 87*(5), 940–971.

Bernasconi, M., Levaggi, R., & Menoncin, F. (2020). Dynamic Tax Evasion with Habit Formation in Consumption. *The Scandinavian Journal of Economics, 122*(3), 966–992.

[6] Obviously, interest in questions of methodology in relation to macroeconomic theory has been a constant theme for many researchers, especially for those belonging to heterodox schools (for a discussion, see King, 2023).

Bilbiie, F. (2020). The New Keynesian Cross. *Journal of Monetary Economics, 114*, 90–108.

Blecker, R. A. (2025). Monopoly, Inequality, and the Economy: Kaleckian Macro Models for Undergraduate Teaching. *Review of Political Economy*, 1–27.

Buiter, W. (2003). James Tobin: An Appreciation of His Contribution to Economics. *The Economic Journal, 113*(491), F585–F631.

Bunting, D. (1989). The Consumption Function 'Paradox'. *Journal of Post Keynesian Economics, 11*(3), 347–359.

Bunting, D. (2001). Keynes's Law and Its Critics. *Journal of Post Keynesian Economics, 24*, 149–163.

Boskin, M., & Sheshinski, E. (1978). Optimal Redistributive Taxation When Individual Welfare Depends upon Relative Income. *The Quarterly Journal of Economics, 92*(4), 589–601.

Boug, P., Cappelen, A., Jansen, E., & Swensen, A. R. (2021). The Consumption Euler Equation or the Keynesian Consumption Function? *Oxford Bulletin of Economics and Statistics, 83*(1), 0305–9049.

Carroll, C., Slacalek, J., Tokuoka, K., & White, M. N. (2017). The Distribution of Wealth and the Marginal Propensity to Consume. *Quantitative Economics, 8*, 977–1020.

Corneo, G. (2002). The Efficient Side of Progressive Income Taxation. *European Economic Review, 46*(7), 1359–1368.

Dow, S. (2023). Keynes on Theorising for Policy. In S. A. Drakopoulos & I. Katselidis (Eds.), *Economic Policy and the History of Economic Thought* (pp. 173–187). Routledge.

Drakopoulos, S. (2021). The Marginalization of Absolute and Relative Income Hypotheses of Consumption and the Role of Fiscal Policy. *The European Journal of the History of Economic Thought, 28*(6), 965–984.

Duesenberry, J. S. (1949). *Income, Saving and the Theory of Consumer Behaviour*. Harvard University Press.

Dutt, A. K. (2003). On Post Walrasian Economics, Macroeconomic Policy, and Heterodox Economics. *International Journal of Political Economy, 33*(2), 47–67.

Earl, P. (2018). Richard H. Thaler: A Nobel Prize for Behavioural Economics. *Review of Political Economy, 30*(2), 107–125.

Earl, P. (2022). *Principles of Behavioral Economics: Bringing Together Old, New and Evolutionary Approaches*. Cambridge University Press.

Edwards, J. (2014). Consumer Power and Market Control: Exploring Consumer Behaviour in Affluent contexts (1946–1980). *European Journal of the History of Economic Thought, 21*, 699–723.

Fazzari, S. (1994–1995). Why Doubt the Effectiveness of Keynesian Fiscal Policy? *Journal of Post Keynesian Economics 17*(2), 231–248.

Foster, J. (2021). The US Consumption Function: A New Perspective. *Journal of Evolutionary Economics, 31*, 773–798.

Frantz, R. (2020). *The Beginnings of Behavioral Economics: Katona, Simon, and Leibenstein's X Efficiency Theory*. Academic Press.

Friedman, M. (1956). The Quantity Theory of Money—A Restatement. In M. Friedman (Ed.), *Studies in the Quantity Theory of Money* (pp. 3–21). University of Chicago Press.

Friedman, M. (1957). *The Consumption Function*. Princeton University Press.

Galbraith, J. K. (1958). *The Affluent Society*. Houghton Mifflin.

Galbraith, J. K. (1967). *The New Industrial State*. Houghton Mifflin.

Gali, J. (2015). *Monetary Policy, Inflation, and the Business Cycle: An Introduction to the new Keynesian Framework and its Applications* (2nd ed.). Princeton University Press.

Hall, R. E. (1978). Stochastic Implications of the Life Cycle-Permanent Income Hypothesis: Theory and Evidence. *Journal of Political Economy, 86*(6), 971–987.

Hamilton, D. (1987). Institutional Economics and Consumption. *Journal of Economic Issues, 21*(4), 1531–1554.

Hein, E. (2023). *Macroeconomics after Kalecki and Keynes: Post-Keynesian Foundations*. Edward Elgar.

Heise, A. (2022). Ideology, Werturteilsfreiheit and Pluralism in Economics. In M. R. Byrialsen, H. Raza, & F. Olesen (Eds.), *Macroeconomic Modelling, Economic Policy and Methodology* (pp. 11–25). Routledge.

Heise, A. (2023). Fiscal Policy after the Crisis: What Role for Fiscal Policy in Times of Crisis, Low Interest Rates and High Public Debts? In S. A. Drakopoulos & I. Katselidis (Eds.), *Economic Policy and the History of Economic Thought* (pp. 245–264). Routledge.

Hemming, R., Kell, M., & Mahfouz, S. (2002). *The Effectiveness of Fiscal Policy in Stimulating Economic Activity: A Review of the Literature*. IMF Working Paper 02/208, Washington DC.

Hoover, K. (2009). Microfoundations and the Ontology of Macroeconomics. In H. Kincaid & D. Ross (Eds.), *The Oxford Handbook of Philosophy of Economics* (pp. 386–409). Oxford University Press.

Hutchison, T. (1964). *"Positive" Economics and Policy Objectives*. Allen and Unwin.

Jappelli, T., & Pistaferri, L. (2014). Fiscal Policy and MPC Heterogeneity. *American Economic Journal: Macroeconomics, 6*(4), 107–136.

Kahneman, D., & Tversky, A. (1979). Prospect Theory: An Analysis of Decision Underrisk. *Econometrica, 47*, 263–291.

Kaplan, G., Moll, B., & Violante, G. (2018). Monetary Policy According to HANK. *American Economic Review, 108*(3), 697–743.

Keen, S. (2011). *Debunking Economics. The Naked Emperor Dethroned?* Second Revised and Expanded Edition. Zed Books.

King, J. (2012). *The Microfoundations Delusion: Metaphor and Dogma in the History of Macroeconomics.* Edward Elgar.
King, J. (2013). An Introduction to Post Keynesian Macroeconomics. *Jahrgang, 39*(4), 485–507.
King, J. (2023). Post Keynesian Methodology. In J. Jespersen, V. Chick, & B. Tieben (Eds.), *Routledge Handbook of Macroeconomic Methodology* (pp. 197–207). Routledge.
Kocherlakota, N. (2022). Stabilization with Fiscal Policy. *Journal of Monetary Economics, 131*, 1–14.
Kosicki, G. (1990). Income Redistribution and Aggregate Consumption: Implications of the Relative Income Model. *The American Economist, 34*(1), 40–44.
Kosobud, R. (1998). Relative Income Hypothesis. In J. Eatwell, M. Milgate, & P. Newman (Eds.), *The New Palgrave: A Dictionary of Economics* (Vol. 4, pp. 134–136). Macmillan.
Krueger, A. (2012). The Rise and Consequences of Inequality in the United States. *Council of Economic Advisers Address*, January 12, 2012.
Kydland, F., & Prescott, E. (1982). Time to Build and Aggregate Fluctuations. *Econometrica, 50*, 1345–1370.
Laidler, D. (2010). Lucas, Keynes, and the Crisis. *Journal of the History of Economic Thought, 32*(1), 39–62.
Lamdin, D. (2008). Galbraith on Advertising, Credit, and Consumption: A Retrospective and Empirical Investigation with Policy Implications. *Review of Political Economy, 20*(4), 595–611.
Lepers, E. (2017). The Neutrality Illusion: Biased Economics, Biased Training, and Biased Monetary Policy. Testing the Role of Ideology on FOMC Voting Behaviour. *New Political Economy, 23*(1), 105–127.
Mantzavinos, C. (2024). *The Constitution of Science.* Cambridge University Press.
Marchionatti, R., & Sella, L. (2017). Is Neo-Walrasian Macroeconom(etr)ics a Dead End? An Assessment of Recent Criticisms of DSGE Models. *Journal of Post Keynesian Economics, 40*(4), 441–469.
McCormick, K. (2018). James Duesenberry as a Practitioner of Behavioural Economics. *Journal of Behavioral Economics for Policy, 2*(1), 3–18.
Menz, J.-O. (2010). Uncertainty, Social Norms and Consumption Theory: Post and New Keynesian Approaches. *Intervention: European Journal of Economics and Economic Policies, 7*(1), 125–146.
Muellbauer, J. (2016). *Macroeconomics and Consumption.* Economics Series Working Papers Paper, No. 811, University of Oxford, Department of Economics, Oxford, UK, pp. 1–37.
Postlewaite, A. (1998). The Social Basis of Interdependent Preferences. *European Economic Review, 42*(3–5), 779–800.

Rabin, M. (2002). A Perspective on Psychology and Economics. *European Economic Review, 46*, 657–685.

Rochon, L.-P. (2023). The Future of Post-Keynesian Economics: Post-Keynesian Economics at 50. *The Journal of Philosophical Economics, 16*, 254–279.

Sent, E. M. (2004). Behavioral Economics: How Psychology Made Its (Limited) Way Back into Economics. *History of Political Economy, 36*, 735–760.

Shefrin, H. & Thaler, R. (1988). The Behavioral Life-cycle Hypothesis. *Economic Inquiry, 26* (4), 609–643.

Snowdon, B., & Vane, H. (2005). *Modern Macroeconomics: Its Origins, Development and Current State*. Edward Elgar.

Skidelsky, R. (1992). *John Maynard Keynes: The Economist as Saviour 1920–1937*. Macmillan.

Solow, R. (2008). The State of Macroeconomics. *Journal of Economic Perspectives, 22*(1), 243–249.

Taylor, L. (2004). *Reconstructing Macroeconomics: Structuralist Proposals and Critiques of the Mainstream*. Harvard University Press.

Thaler, R. (1980). Toward a Positive Theory of Consumer Choice. *Journal of Economic Behavior and Organization, 1*(1), 39–60.

Thaler, R. (1999). Mental Accounting Matters. *Journal of Behavioral Decision Making, 12*(3), 183–206.

Thaler, R. (2015). *Misbehaving*. W.W. Norton and Company.

Tobin, J. (1956). The Interest-Elasticity of Transactions Demand for Cash. *Review of Economics and Statistics, 38*, 241–247.

Tobin, J. (1972). Friedman's Theoretical Framework. *Journal of Political Economy, 80*(5), 319–337.

Tobin, J. (1981). The Monetarist Counter-Revolution Today—An Appraisal. *The Economic Journal, 91*(361), 29–42.

Todorova, Z. (2014). Consumption as a Social Process. *Journal of Economic Issues, 48*(3), 663–678.

Trezzini, A. (2012). Relative Consumption vs. Permanent Income: The Crisis of the Theory of the Social Significance of Consumption. *Journal of the History of Economic Thought, 34*(3), 355–377.

Truyts, T. (2010). Social Status in Economic Theory. *Journal of Economic Surveys, 24*(1), 137–169.

Index[1]

A

Absolute income hypothesis (AIH), 3, 5, 6, 29, 30, 39, 40, 45, 45n5, 46, 48, 56, 64, 69, 107, 139, 142, 149
Ackley, G., 39, 41
Agent-Based Models (ABM), 98
Agent representative, *see* Representative agent
Agents, 97
  forward-looking, 2, 3, 6, 8, 45, 70, 73, 84, 89, 100, 140, 141
  heterogeneous, 97, 98
  optimising, 2, 4, 8, 116, 140–141, 147, 149
  rational, 8, 73, 127, 139–141, 146, 147, 149
Aggregate demand, ix, 1, 29, 34, 72, 83, 96, 111, 127, 140, 142, 144, 145, 147
Aggregation problem, 127
Ando, A., 79, 81
Animal spirits, 27, 28, 28n6, 114n7
Arrow, K., 59, 59n5, 127–129
Asset
  pricing, 99
  switching, 79
Average propensity to consume (APC), 29, 31, 32, 34, 39, 41–44, 46, 56–59, 79, 82, 107, 140, 141

B

Bandwagon effect, 61
Baumol, W., 125
Behavioural economics
  new, 8, 140, 145–147, 146n3, 149
  old, 146n3
Bentham, J., 26, 132
Bilbiie, F., 96, 97, 143
Blanchard, O., 93, 95, 96, 125
Blaug, M., 123, 130
Borrowing, 6, 32, 73, 83, 93, 94, 96, 97, 100
Boumans, M., 130, 130n8

[1] Note: Page numbers followed by 'n' refer to notes.

S. A. Drakopoulos, *The Consumption Function in Economics*, https://doi.org/10.1007/978-3-032-15958-8

Bounded rationality, 114
Brady, D., 53n1, 80n3
Brown, T., 60
Brumberg, R., 2, 6, 65, 71, 72, 76, 76n2, 81, 84, 90, 107, 141, 147
Budget
  line, 74, 75
  studies, 41, 42, 57
Bunting, D., 3, 34, 45, 47, 79, 84, 140, 141
Burns, J., 80n3
Business cycle, 41, 42, 43n3, 57, 58, 110–112, 126

C
Cambridge school, 105, 113
Capacity utilisation, 111
Capitalism, 4, 33n8, 110, 116
Capitalists, 109–114, 110n4, 116
Carroll, C., 80, 91n1, 92, 93, 98, 122–124, 126, 128, 143, 144
Catching up with the Joneses, 99
Certainty equivalence, 122
Classical political economy, 1, 109, 130
Clower, R., 72, 105, 106, 106n1
Coldberger, A., 41
Commons, J., 11, 16, 16n7
Consumer(s), 2, 5, 11, 15–18, 28, 31, 34, 35, 40, 41n1, 43, 46, 47, 51–55, 57, 59, 60, 61n6, 62–64, 69, 71, 73–75, 77–82, 84, 90, 92–96, 99, 106, 121, 122, 124, 125, 132, 140, 145, 146, 148n4, 149, 150
Consumption
  autonomous, 31–33, 41, 111
  conspicuous, 5, 12, 14–16, 19, 54, 62
  irreversibility of, 15, 16
  permanent, 81, 82
  relative, 52, 59, 63, 64, 72, 83, 115, 141
  transitory, 81, 107
Coordination, 106, 108
Cross-section data, 39, 40
Cunynghame, H., 11, 61
Cyclical fluctuations, 58

D
Davidson, P., 115, 131
Davis, J., 129, 130, 130n8
Davis, T., 46
Deaton, A., 4, 76, 79, 80, 90, 92, 115
Debt, 122, 142
Deficit, 110n4, 122
De Grauwe, P., 128
Demand
  aggregate, ix, 1, 29, 34, 72, 83, 96, 111, 127, 140, 142, 144, 145, 147
  management, 142–144
  theory, 6, 51, 53–55, 72
Demonstration effect, 6, 51–54, 56, 62
Denis, A., 124, 129
D'Ippoliti, C., 111
Dolde, W., 107, 108
Dual-decision hypothesis, 106
Duesenberry, J., 2, 3, 6–8, 15, 19, 45, 48, 51–65, 69–72, 79, 83, 84, 115, 139–141
Dutt, A., 132, 144
Dynamic Stochastic General Equilibrium (DSGE) theory, 3, 7, 90, 95–96, 95n2, 96n3, 100, 105, 115, 121, 122, 124–126, 128, 129, 143, 149

E
Earl, P., 146
Econometrics, 6, 39–41, 42n2, 43, 46–48
Economic growth, 1, 19, 43n4, 109, 111–113, 116

Edgeworth, F. Y., 26, 26n3
Employment, ix, 1, 3, 5, 26, 76, 78, 140, 142
Emulation, 14, 15, 19, 54, 111
Equity premium puzzle, 93, 99
Euler equation, 90–93, 91n1, 95, 98, 100, 105, 108, 125, 142
Excess sensitivity of consumption puzzle, 92
Expectations
  adaptive, 70, 81, 90
  rational, 3, 6, 70, 84, 90–92, 95, 100, 115, 122, 131, 142, 148n4, 149

F
Fallacy of composition, 28, 28n7, 123
Fertility decline, 62
Financial crisis, 96, 96n3, 100, 128, 143
Fiscal policy, 1, 3, 5, 7, 25, 33, 35, 83, 97, 107, 116, 139–145, 144n2, 149, 150
Fisher, I., 2, 6, 26, 29, 65, 69, 70, 73–75, 77, 80, 84, 89, 93, 94, 107
Fishman, L., 46
Foley, C., 11
Following behaviour, 16, 143, 150
Forward-looking
  agents, 2, 3, 6, 8, 45, 70, 73, 84, 89, 100, 140, 141
  consumers, 73, 80, 145, 149
Friedman, M., 3, 6, 41, 42, 45, 53n1, 59n5, 64, 65, 69–72, 76n2, 80–84, 80n3, 90, 95, 123, 123n2, 125, 142, 144, 147
Friedman, R., 53n1, 59n5, 80n3

G
Galbraith, J. K., 16, 61n6, 64, 132, 145
General equilibrium, 90, 95, 97, 122, 124, 126
Gilboy, Elizabeth Waterman, 19, 19n10, 20
Goodwin, R., 112, 131
Government expenditure, 1, 32–34, 116, 140, 145
Great Depression, 43
Gross Domestic Product (GDP), ix, 1, 43

H
Habit(s), 13, 14n3, 28, 52, 55, 98–100, 143, 150
Hahn, F., 128
Hamilton, D., 16, 132, 145
Hamilton, W., 13
Hands, W., 96, 124, 126–128
Hand-to mouth
  agents, 96, 97
  consumers, 93, 95
  households, 97
HANK models, 97, 100, 105
Hansen, A., 40
Harcourt, G., 109
Hartley, J., 96, 123, 124, 126, 127
Hedonism
  Benthamite, 26
  philosophy of, 26
  psychological, 12, 26
Hedonistic, 12, 13, 26, 27
Heilbroner, R., 132, 133
Hendry, D., 95, 95n2, 125
Heterodox
  macroeconomics, 4, 7, 108, 122, 130–133
  schools, 84, 114n6, 140, 144–145, 150n6
Heterogeneous households, *see* Agents
Hicks, J., 39, 40, 123
High-income group(s), 34
Hirsch, F., 62n7
Hobson, J., 2
Hodgson, G., 13n1, 129, 130, 132

Homo economicus, 78
Hoover, K., 51, 90, 126, 128, 129, 147
Households, 3, 15, 32, 34, 43, 47, 51–55, 58, 62, 79, 93, 95–97, 98n4, 100, 106, 107, 113, 115, 125, 126, 141–145, 149
Hynes, A., 4, 45, 47, 48, 51, 52, 53n1, 76n2, 107

I
Ideology, 147–148, 148n5
Idiosyncratic income shocks, 97
Income
  current, 3, 25, 29, 31, 35, 52–54, 57, 58, 60, 76n2, 78–81, 83, 93–95, 141
  distribution, 35, 45, 56, 57, 59, 109, 111–113, 116, 127, 144n2
  elasticity of consumption, 44
  expected, 78–80, 92, 95, 111, 141, 142
  family, 41, 56, 123
  redistribution, 34, 35, 59, 140, 141
  transitory, 80, 81
Independent preferences, 53, 99
Inflation, 116, 139, 142, 143
Instincts and habits, 12, 13
Institutionalism/ist, 2, 5, 11, 12, 15–17, 19, 20, 55, 111, 132
Interdependent preferences, 59n4, 72, 99, 99n5
Intertemporal choice, theory of, 6, 69, 73–75, 78, 95, 133
Investment, ix, 1, 30, 32–35, 43, 83, 109, 110, 112, 114n7, 140, 141
IS-LM model, 40, 123

J
Janssen, M., 124, 128, 129
Jevons, W. S., 26

K
Kahn, R., 131
Kaldor, N., 3, 7, 105, 106, 111–114, 116, 131
Kalecki, M., 3, 7, 105, 106, 108–112, 114, 116, 130, 131
Katona, G., 6, 52, 63, 64, 64n8, 146n3
Keeping up (or Keep up) with the Joneses, 16, 54, 55, 98–100, 143
Keynes, J. M., ix, 1–8, 11–20, 25–35, 39–42, 44, 45, 47, 48, 51–53, 58, 63, 64, 64n8, 69–72, 78–80, 83, 84, 89, 105, 106, 106n1, 108–111, 114–116, 114n7, 123, 123n2, 132, 139–141, 148, 149
  psychological law of consumption, 19, 19n10, 71
Keynesian cross, 97, 143
King, J., 64, 64n8, 89, 96, 109, 110, 110n4, 114–116, 122, 124, 131, 145, 147
Kirman, A., 96, 127
Klein, L., 39, 41
Kuznets paradox, 2, 5, 39–48
Kuznets, S., 2, 5, 6, 39–48, 51, 52, 55, 57, 69
Kyrk, H., 2, 5, 11, 12, 17–20, 52, 63

L
Laidler, D., 89, 125, 130, 143
Lawson, T., 27, 27n4, 115, 129
Leibenstein, H., 6, 51–65
Leijonhufvud, A., 106, 106n1, 128
Life-cycle hypothesis (LCH), 2, 6, 65, 69, 70, 76–80, 83, 84, 89, 141
Linguanti, F., 111
Liquidity constraints, 79, 83, 93, 107
Living standards, 19, 45
Loss aversion, 146
Low-income group(s), 34, 43
Lucas critique, 70, 124, 126

Lucas, R., 3, 69, 70, 90, 124, 126, 127, 130

M

Malthus, T., 1, 2
Mankiw, G., 92–94, 96, 125
Marginal
  propensity to consume (MPC), 1, 25, 29–35, 39–41, 43, 44, 46, 58, 59, 78, 79, 81, 82, 97, 111, 115, 140, 141, 143–145
  propensity to save (MPS), 111, 113
  rate of substitution, 74
Marginalism, 5, 12–14
Marshall, A., 12, 26, 26n3, 126
Marx, K., 52
Mayer, T., 47
McMahon, T., 19, 20
Meade, J., 61, 106
Meghir, C., 71, 80–82
Mental accounting, 146
Methodological individualism, 4, 7, 121, 122, 128–130, 132, 133, 149
Microfoundations, 4, 7, 28n7, 70, 89, 96, 108, 115, 122–128, 126n5, 130–133, 130n8, 147, 149
Milberg, W., 132, 133
Mill, J.S., 15n5, 52
Mitchell, W., 11, 15, 17, 42
Modigliani, F., 2, 6, 40, 45, 59, 60, 65, 71, 72, 76, 76n2, 77, 79, 81, 84, 90, 107, 113–115, 141, 147
Monetarism, 26n1, 107, 142, 144, 147
Monetary policy, 99, 100, 106, 116, 140, 142, 143
Monopolistic competition, 122
Monopoly, 110
Morgenstern, O., 72
Muellbauer, J., 3, 95, 95n2, 122, 123n1, 125, 128, 143
Multiplier
  fiscal, 33n9, 97, 140, 143, 149
  investment, 34, 83, 140
  Keynesian, 25, 33, 33n9, 97
  tax, 1, 30, 34, 140, 143n1
Muth, J., 90

N

Neoclassical economics, 5, 12–14, 109, 110, 132
New Classical Macroeconomics, 3, 26n1, 69, 126, 147

O

Ogburn, W., 15, 16, 16n6
Old Keynesian school, 140, 144–145
Output, ix, 1, 3, 5, 26, 43, 112, 123, 139, 140, 142, 143, 144n2

P

Paradigm, 65, 70, 84, 97
Pareto criterion, 59, 141
Pasinetti, L., 4, 7, 105, 106, 111–114, 114n5, 116, 131
Patinkin, D., 106n1
Peixot, J., 19, 20
Perfect foresight, 122, 123, 148n4
Permanent-income hypothesis (PIH), 3, 6, 7, 64, 65, 69, 70, 80–84, 89, 95, 139, 142, 149
Pignalosa, D., 4, 16, 30, 41, 71, 72, 91–93, 95, 98–100, 124
Pigou, A.C., 26, 52, 59, 59n5, 61
Positional goods, 59n4, 62n7, 141
Post Keynesian school, 4, 7, 105, 106, 109, 114
Precautionary saving, 18, 115, 145
Present bias, 146
Prices, 57, 62, 74, 93, 123n1, 124
Probability, 27, 28, 115, 122

Profits, 109–114, 110n4, 116, 124, 145
Property, 11, 14, 95, 112, 113, 127, 131
Psychology, 12, 13, 26, 51, 60–62, 64, 72, 89

Q
Quantity theory of money, 142

R
Ramsey, F., 73
Random walk, 3, 6, 7, 90–92, 100, 124, 142
Ratchet effect, 6, 51, 52, 55
Rate of interest, 29, 74, 81, 91
Rational
  choice, 16, 73, 89, 146
  consumer, 2, 73, 79, 149
Real business cycle models/theory (RBC), 122, 126
Reid, M., 76n2, 80n3
Representative agent, 3, 4, 6, 7, 90, 95–98, 100, 105, 108, 116, 121, 122, 124–129, 131–133, 139, 144, 149
Representative Agent New Keynesian (RANK) models, 3, 97, 100, 143
Retirement consumption puzzle, 93
Risk, 27, 122, 123n1, 149
Robbins, L., 126
Robinson, J., 109, 112, 131
Rule of thumb consumers, 93, 94

S
Samuelson, P., 39, 41, 41n1, 113, 114
Savings, ix, 1, 12, 15, 16n6, 17–20, 28, 29, 32, 41–45, 55, 57, 59, 59n5, 73, 74, 76, 79, 80, 93, 99, 106, 107, 107n2, 109, 111–116, 145–147
Sawyer, M., 109, 110, 116, 131, 145
Schackle, G.L.S., 59
Scitovsky, T., 61n6
Self-control, 146
Self-esteem, 17, 18
Self-interest, 70
Selfish, 13, 14
Simon, H., 114, 146n3
Smith, A., 15n4, 15n5, 52, 131
Smithies, A., 45
Snob effect, 61, 62
Social
  comparisons, 14, 52, 53, 72
  influence group, 63
  psychology, 51, 60–62, 89
  ranking, 14
  status, 6, 14, 15, 17, 52, 55, 60–64
Socioeconomic classes, 105, 109, 111, 112, 131
Solow, R., 125, 148, 148n4
Spanos, A., 46
Sraffa, P., 131
S.R. man, 61
Stabilisation, 4, 5, 7, 25, 35, 100, 107, 116, 139–141, 143, 144
Status goods, 15, 62
Stigler, G., 72
Stiglitz, J., 3, 96, 122, 127, 128
Stone, R., 42
Stylized facts, 46

T
TANK models, 7, 90, 96, 97
Tax
  cuts, 79, 141, 145
  optimal, 59, 141
  policy, 99, 140, 141, 145

Taxation
  multiplier, 1, 30, 33n9, 34, 140, 143n1
  progressive, 34, 35, 59, 140, 141
Taylor, L., 89, 128, 130, 142
Thaler, R., 93, 146, 146n3, 147
Thomas, J., 16n6, 19, 47
Time preference, 91
Time-series data, 39, 40, 42, 43, 45, 46, 48, 57
Tobin, J., 3, 7, 45n5, 105–108, 116, 125, 128, 144, 147, 148

U
Uncertainty, 3, 16, 27, 27n4, 27n5, 28, 30, 78, 79, 83, 114, 114n7, 115, 122, 123n1, 131, 132, 144, 144n2, 145
Underconsumption, 1, 2, 99
Unemployment, 2, 29, 35, 106, 116, 144n2, 145
Utilitarianism, 13, 26, 26n2
Utility
  expected, 27, 28, 121, 123, 132
  maximisation, 27, 28, 73, 96, 106, 132
  theory, 2, 5, 6, 26–28, 45, 100, 106, 121, 132

V
Veblen effect, 61, 62
Veblen, T., 2, 5, 6, 11–20, 26, 51, 52, 54, 55, 63, 132, 145

W
Wages, 29, 52, 106, 109, 111–113, 116, 124, 145
Walrasian general equilibrium, 126
Wealth, 2, 11, 14, 52, 78–80, 91–95, 97, 107, 107n2, 123, 142
Wealth decumulation puzzle, 93
Workers, 16, 29, 109, 111–114, 116
Wren-Lewis, S., 125

Y
Young, A., 126, 131

FSC
www.fsc.org
MIX
Papier | Fördert gute Waldnutzung
FSC® C083411

Kolibri 360 GmbH
Ferdinand-Jühlke-Straße 7
99095 Erfurt, Deutschland
produktsicherheit@kolibri360.de